ANXIETY

TIPS AND STRATEGIES TO **MANAGE ANXIETY, BUILD RESILIENCE**, AND **FOSTER EMOTIONAL WELL-BEING**

DR. LEIGH BAGWELL

NATIONAL CENTER for
YOUTH ISSUES

15-MINUTE FOCUS
Anxiety Workbook: Tips and Strategies to Manage Anxiety, Build Resilience, and Foster Emotional Well-Being

1

Duplication and Copyright

No part of this publication may be reproduced, stored in a retrieval system, or transmitted in any form by any means, electronic, mechanical, photocopy, video or audio recording, or otherwise without prior written permission from the publisher, except for all worksheets and activities which may be reproduced for a specific group or class. Reproduction for an entire school or school district is prohibited.

NATIONAL CENTER for
YOUTH ISSUES

P.O. Box 22185
Chattanooga, TN 37422-2185
423.899.5714 • 866.318.6294
fax: 423.899.4547 • www.ncyi.org

ISBN: 9781953945839

© 2024 National Center for Youth Issues, Chattanooga, TN

All rights reserved.

Written by: Dr. Leigh Bagwell

Published by National Center for Youth Issues

Printed in the U.S.A. • March 2024

Third party links are accurate at the time of publication, but may change over time.

The information in this book is designed to provide helpful information on the subjects discussed and is not intended to be used, nor should it be used, to diagnose or treat any mental health or medical condition. For diagnosis or treatment of any mental health or medical issue, consult a licensed counselor, psychologist, or physician. The publisher and author are not responsible for any specific mental or physical health needs that may require medical supervision, and are not liable for any damages or negative consequences from any treatment, action, application, or preparation, to any person reading or following the information in this book. References are provided for informational purposes only and do not constitute endorsement of any websites or other sources.

2

15-MINUTE FOCUS
Anxiety Workbook: Tips and Strategies to Manage Anxiety, Build Resilience, and Foster Emotional Well-Being

Dedication

Anxiety is one of the greatest needs expressed by our students. They experience levels of worry and fear that the adults around them often did not know until we were much older and had many more tools to process and manage those big feelings. Whether their anxiety interrupts their learning or cripples their daily functioning, our students need a variety of supports to name, handle, and conquer the experiences that steal their joy and peace.

To the school counselors, teachers, caregivers, administrators, educators, social workers, coaches, mental health providers, concerned adults…to all of you who invest in the mental wellness of our young people, I see you. Thank you for doing your part to build up our children and youth. Thank you for being a safe space for the students in your world to share their fears and worries. The work you do matters! It is important! It is making a difference, even when you cannot see it!

The work is hard, but you are not alone. This workbook is my effort to partner with you all as you support your students. It is my hope that you can add the strategies and activities included here to your toolbox for working with the children in your care. Together, let's continue to educate, equip, and empower our students so that when they experience anxiety they can understand it, access coping skills to manage it, and apply proven strategies to decrease its impact on them.

I dedicate this book to all of you, and the children you have served. And the many more you will continue to serve!

Investing Together,

Dr. Leigh

15-MINUTE FOCUS
Anxiety Workbook: Tips and Strategies to Manage Anxiety, Build Resilience, and Foster Emotional Well-Being

3

Table of Contents

 = Elementary   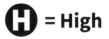 = Middle    = High

4

15-MINUTE FOCUS
Anxiety Workbook: Tips and Strategies to Manage Anxiety, Build Resilience, and Foster Emotional Well-Being

15-MINUTE FOCUS
Anxiety Workbook: Tips and Strategies to Manage Anxiety, Build Resilience, and Foster Emotional Well-Being

5

6

15-MINUTE FOCUS
Anxiety Workbook: Tips and Strategies to Manage Anxiety, Build Resilience, and Foster Emotional Well-Being

8

15-MINUTE FOCUS
Anxiety Workbook: Tips and Strategies to Manage Anxiety, Build Resilience, and Foster Emotional Well-Being

**See page 206 for information about
Downloadable Resources and Templates.**

15-MINUTE FOCUS
Anxiety Workbook: Tips and Strategies to Manage Anxiety, Build Resilience, and Foster Emotional Well-Being

9

Purpose of this Book

After writing *15-Minute Focus: Anxiety: Worry, Stress and Fear,*[1] the feedback I received from school counselors, teachers, and caregivers was overwhelming. Students are experiencing high levels of stress that are interrupting their learning, their relationships, and in some cases, their daily functioning. Concerned educators expressed a need for specific strategies to support students that are easy to implement. Given the increased needs, educators do not have time to research proven methods for helping children with anxiety. They want access to trusted resources so they can spend their time helping students.

I developed this workbook as a companion to my first book on anxiety. *Anxiety: Worry, Stress and Fear* provides a foundation for understanding the experience of anxiety. General strategies for how various educators can serve students experiencing anxiety provide a structure for schools to create a comprehensive approach to supporting students with anxiety. This workbook includes activities, ideas, and interventions designed from evidence-based practices shown to be effective for students experiencing anxiety.

It is my hope that this workbook offers an opportunity to collaborate to support the students enduring anxiety in your school community.

10

15-MINUTE FOCUS
Anxiety Workbook: Tips and Strategies to Manage Anxiety, Build Resilience, and Foster Emotional Well-Being

How to Use this Book

Effectively managing and reducing anxiety begins with a broad understanding of general anxiety. This workbook is designed to support individual, classroom, and school-wide efforts to address anxiety in your school community. I provide developmentally differentiated lessons, activities, and resources to help students and adults establish a strong foundation of knowledge of anxiety. The emphases of these interventions range from education and awareness to targeted individual interventions. Universal prevention and intervention activities, as well as targeted individual strategies, can be effective in reducing anxiety in children and adolescents.[2]

Subsequent chapters build on the understanding of general anxiety and focus on specific anxiety or specific triggers of anxiety such as test anxiety, social anxiety, and anxiety related to family issues. The resources in these chapters are narrow in scope; however, they can be enhanced by those presented in Chapters 1 and 2.

The strategies and tools include:

- Research-based information about the type of anxiety discussed.
- Student examples.
- Lesson plans and activities that can be delivered by the classroom teacher, the school counselor as part of the school counselor program, or through an advisory program.
- Individual counseling interventions.
- Classroom accommodations, considerations, or modifications classroom teachers can use to help students to manage or reduce their anxiety.
- Information for caregivers to bridge the student support between school and home.

The individual counseling interventions should be delivered by a school counselor or school social worker. Because these are designed as counseling interventions, I recommend that the school counselor or school social worker provide consultation before another school staff member utilizes these interventions.

See page 206 for information about Downloadable Resources and Templates.

15-MINUTE FOCUS
Anxiety Workbook: Tips and Strategies to Manage Anxiety, Build Resilience, and Foster Emotional Well-Being

11

CHAPTER ONE

What is Anxiety?

Anxiety is the excessive concern about a potential triggering event or perceived threat to one's safety. That safety can be physical, emotional, or social.

Anxiety is a normal part of life. We all have experienced anxiety at some point, felt our pulse race, breath become shallow and quick, and muscles start to shake and tremor. Our bodies tell us that we are in danger and need to act quickly to maintain our safety. Or we could be preparing to do something important, and those nerves remind us how much we care about being successful. Anxiety is uncomfortable, however, for many adults and children, and we can use coping skills to manage and reduce the uneasiness. Each event is an opportunity to reinforce the idea that we have the capacity to face difficult challenges and overcome them.

For a growing number of our students, what has been typical anxiety is changing. There has been a significant increase of anxiety in students and adults. Prior to the COVID-19 pandemic, there was a noticeable rise in students reporting feelings of anxiety and worry. However, the impact of the pandemic on schools and communities left students and adults showing a sharp increase in anxiety.[3] Navigating changes in learning environments, increased isolation, a greater dependence on social media for social interaction, fear associated with the unknown, and conflicting information about the pandemic left children experiencing higher levels of anxiety and worry about their physical, emotional, and social safety. Additionally, the increase of violence in and around our school campuses has left students, their families, and their communities in heightened states of anxiety and concern. The continued occurrences of school shootings and the challenges in effectively reducing the threats to our schools and communities have intensified anxiety experienced by children and adults.

As families navigate the challenges of maintaining households, balancing work and leisure, and planning for the future, many students are assuming more adult responsibilities to help make ends meet. They are caring for siblings, providing basic needs, and working to contribute financially while carrying the weight of schoolwork, maintaining social connections, and discovering who they are and what they want to do in their lives. Many of these students are still developing and growing and may not have the cognitive, social, and physical skills to successfully manage all they are asked. These complex situations are fraught with anxiety and worry.

12

15-MINUTE FOCUS
Anxiety Workbook: Tips and Strategies to Manage Anxiety, Build Resilience, and Foster Emotional Well-Being

The conditions above are shifting what is considered "normal." Chronic anxiety and worry that last for long periods of time are becoming the new baseline "normal." Students and adults are experiencing anxiety more often and with more intensity. There are still events that lead to acute anxiety, moments of severe anxiety and panic. But many of our students are suffering with anxiety that interrupts their learning and ability to navigate life's challenges. We can support them with interventions, such as helping them understand anxiety, teaching them coping skills, providing counseling, and connecting them and their families to resources for additional support when necessary. The information, activities, and resources included in this book are designed to provide educators, mental health providers, caregivers, and youth-serving professionals tools to confront anxiety in your school communities.

Challenges in Supporting Students Experiencing Anxiety

One challenge in supporting students who are struggling is that anxiety is often an internalizing disorder. Students can often keep their distressing thoughts and feelings to themselves. There are several reasons why a student may not share their feelings with others:

- They may not have an adequate vocabulary or the language skills to clearly articulate their feelings.
- They may be afraid that their feelings will get them into trouble.
- They may not believe that there are helpful solutions to their anxiety.
- They believe that their anxiety is a problem and may want to protect their caregivers, or even teachers from having to take on one more thing.
- They may not have a positive relationship with an adult they trust.

Students can internalize their anxiety through:

- Worrying about things before they happen.
- Constant worries or concerns about family, school, friends, or activities.
- Repetitive, unwanted thoughts (obsessions) or actions (compulsions).
- Fears of embarrassment or making mistakes.
- Low self-esteem and lack of self-confidence.

Another challenge is that students have access to so much more information today. They process a significant amount of material in a very short amount of time. Many students have not developed the cognitive abilities and emotional maturity to effectively handle all that information. Brain science tells us that executive functioning skills are not fully developed until students reach their early twenties. Regulating emotions and self-control are at the core of executive functioning.

All this information, and the inability to manage it in a healthy manner, creates many more opportunities for our young people to compare themselves to others, and we know that comparison is the thief of joy. Their joy has been replaced with fear. Students experience fear of:

- Missing out
- Being popular
- Not being popular

15-MINUTE FOCUS
Anxiety Workbook: Tips and Strategies to Manage Anxiety, Build Resilience, and Foster Emotional Well-Being

13

- Being wrong
- Competing with others, even globally
- Looking the right way
- Measuring up
- Having the right friends
- Making the right decisions
- Being bullied
- Not being enough

Biology and environment can present another challenge to supporting students experiencing anxiety. Some students may be more susceptible to anxiety. Biological, psychological, and environmental factors can put children at greater risk. Because anxiety is rooted in the brain, the way that a student's brain is wired may contribute to anxiousness. Childrens' temperaments and personalities may also heighten their propensity to experience anxiety and early childhood trauma. Even having anxious caregivers can make students more vulnerable. Anxiety has also been identified as a potential side effect of medications.

Educators, caregivers, and mental health professionals must partner to overcome these challenges to meet our students' needs. Schools have been identified as a strategic and effective setting for addressing anxiety in children and youth. Schools provide unique opportunities to identify students experiencing anxiety and teach them skills that can be transferred in various situations, for example, test anxiety, social anxiety, etc.[4] Integrating universal and targeted interventions for anxiety into the larger systems of support encourages collaboration that can lead to positive outcomes for students and the school community.

Anxiety in Neurodivergent Students

Neurodivergence is a non-medical term that describes a category of conditions and diagnoses in which a person's brain works differently than what is considered typical. Neurodivergence can refer to both learning and sensory challenges. Students with diagnoses of Attention Deficit/Hyperactivity Disorder (ADHD), Autism Spectrum Disorder (ASD), Obsessive Compulsive Disorder (OCD), Dyslexia, and Sensory Processing Disorders often are described as neurodivergent.[5] Given that anxiety is a physiological response that occurs in the brain, it is important to consider how our neurodivergent students may experience anxiety and adjustments to supports that are necessary to meet their unique needs.

Between 25–50 percent of children with ADHD also have clinical anxiety, which leads to more challenges with behavior, daily functioning, and academic performance than students with only ADHD. These students also tend to struggle more socially and lack strong social connections with their peers.[6] Anxiety can intensify ADHD symptoms, creating challenges in navigating social situations, an inability to meet academic expectations, increased clinginess with a parent or trusted adult, intensified sensitivity to typical stimuli, and distress in response to change or uncertainty.[7] Cognitive Behavioral Therapy (CBT) has been an effective approach for addressing anxiety for all students, including those with neurodivergent conditions.[8] Historically, students with ADHD participated in social skills intervention; however, for those students with both ADHD and anxiety, interventions specifically for anxiety have proven more effective and enduring.[9]

Social anxiety is common in students diagnosed with either ADHD or ASD. Research is unclear as to whether social anxiety develops because of the ADHD or ASD or is part of the organic physiological makeup of the student; regardless, the student bears the impact of carrying both conditions. These students are at a greater risk of being bullied, so particular attention should be given to providing supports to proactively address this concern. As is common with all who struggle with social anxiety, these students lack meaningful connections with their peers. Once again, there is positive evidence that CBT has helped students diagnosed with social anxiety and either ADHD or ASD to reduce their anxiety. Interventions focused on emotional regulation, development of interpersonal skills, and bullying prevention have all shown positive outcomes as well.[10]

Anxiety is one of the most common dual diagnoses with ASD, with approximately 40 percent of students diagnosed with ASD meeting the criteria for an anxiety disorder, and as many as 84 percent having subclinical symptoms of anxiety. Frequent forms of anxiety include specific phobias, Generalized Anxiety Disorder, Separation Anxiety Disorder, social anxiety, and OCD.[11] These students often experience intensified symptoms of ASD as well as tantrums, aggression, and self-injury. Because of their challenges in communication, they are less likely to express their anxiety in productive ways. Anxiety in students with ASD may also manifest in restlessness, inability to relax, increased uneasiness in social situations, distress when separated from trusted adults, and difficulty sleeping.

There is some evidence that higher-functioning and older students with ASD have increased levels of anxiety. This may be, in part, due to the higher-order cognitive and developmental skills (such as worry, predicting, and imaging) that are known to feed anxiety. These students may also have increased social interactions which could lead to greater likelihood of challenges that trigger their anxiety. Strong data suggests that addressing anxiety in students with ASD can reduce the impairment they experience from the core ASD symptoms.[12] As previously mentioned, CBT is an effective approach for reducing symptoms of anxiety, in addition to regular physical activity or participation in a sport.[13] Interestingly, one study found that students who felt that they were different from their peers reported feeling safe and supported in music classes, which could provide additional possible interventions for our neurodivergent students who experience anxiety.[14]

15-MINUTE FOCUS
Anxiety Workbook: Tips and Strategies to Manage Anxiety, Build Resilience, and Foster Emotional Well-Being

15

Common Symptoms of Anxiety

PHYSICAL SYMPTOMS

- ☐ Increased heart rate
- ☐ Tense muscles
- ☐ Increased blood pressure
- ☐ Excessive sweating
- ☐ Rapid breathing
- ☐ Headaches
- ☐ Nausea
- ☐ Digestive issues
- ☐ Feeling jittery or lightheaded
- ☐ Hot face
- ☐ Clammy hands
- ☐ Dry mouth

EMOTIONAL SYMPTOMS

- ☐ Feeling afraid, worried, or nervous
- ☐ Constant worries or concerns about family, school, friends, or activities
- ☐ Repetitive, unwanted thoughts or actions
- ☐ Fears of embarrassment or making mistakes
- ☐ Low self-esteem
- ☐ Lack of self-confidence
- ☐ Poor sleep
- ☐ Crying

BEHAVIORAL SYMPTOMS

- ☐ Refusing to talk
- ☐ Clinging to caregivers, siblings, or trusted adults
- ☐ Acting scared or upset
- ☐ Startling easily
- ☐ Missing school
- ☐ Refusing to do things
- ☐ Avoiding people
- ☐ Tantrums

What Is Anxiety?

ELEMENTARY

LESSON LENGTH	25 minutes
OBJECTIVES	• Students will understand what anxiety is and how it can affect them. • Students will identify common triggers of anxiety.
MATERIALS	• Definition of Anxiety Coloring Sheet (Elementary) • Colored pencils, markers, or crayons

5 MINUTES

Introduction

- Begin the lesson by asking students if they have ever felt worried or scared before.
- Introduce the definition of anxiety:

  Anxiety is a feeling of worry or fear that everyone experiences from time to time. Anxiety comes from fear. It could be a fear of letting someone else down, a fear of letting ourselves down, or a fear associated with a threat to our physical, emotional, or social safety.

- Have students echo a phrase such as, ***"Anxiety is worry and fear."***
- Explain that anxiety can let us know that we care about something, and we might be worried that we will not do a good job. For example:

  You might get nervous and worried before you perform in front of an audience. You want to do well, and it is common to feel some anxiety because you are afraid you might forget the words or miss a note.

  Sometimes we feel anxiety because we feel like we are in danger and could get hurt. We are afraid of getting physically hurt, having our feelings hurt, or even having our friendships or reputations hurt. An example is when we hear a lot of thunder in a storm or even a tornado siren. We might feel some anxiety because we are afraid we could get hurt in a storm.

- Allow students to ask questions and assess for understanding. Have students echo, ***"Anxiety is worry and fear."***

15-MINUTE FOCUS
Anxiety Workbook: Tips and Strategies to Manage Anxiety, Build Resilience, and Foster Emotional Well-Being

17

What Makes Us Anxious?

- Divide the class into small groups and provide each group with a large sheet of paper and markers. You may also use technology tools if they are available.

- Instruct each group to brainstorm and write down different situations that may make them feel anxious (i.e., starting a new school year, taking a test, speaking in front of the class). For older elementary students, you can ask groups to come up with a trigger to represent each letter of the alphabet or give each group a setting (such as school, home, ball field, mall, etc.) and identify triggers that may happen there.

- After ten minutes, have each group share their ideas with the class. As groups share their anxiety triggers, allow students to identify whether they feel anxiety when those events occur. This reinforces that anxiety is a normal part of life and reassures students that everyone experiences it; however, they can be triggered by different things.

  Learning what triggers our anxiety will help us to control and reduce it. We are going to learn coping skills that will help us to manage and decrease our anxiety.

  Sometimes, though, our anxiety gets intense and keeps us from doing the things that we need to do (like learn and take care of ourselves) or things that we enjoy (like playing with friends or participating in sports). When that happens, it is important that we ask our trusted adults for help.

- Ask students to identify their trusted adults.

Wrap Up & Assessment

- Ask students to echo: *"Anxiety is worry and fear."*
- Ask students to share one thing that triggers their anxiety.
- Distribute the **Definition of Anxiety Coloring Sheet (Elementary)** and the **colored pencils, markers, or crayons**.

15-MINUTE FOCUS
Anxiety Workbook: Tips and Strategies to Manage Anxiety, Build Resilience, and Foster Emotional Well-Being

19

MIDDLE

LESSON LENGTH	40 minutes
OBJECTIVES	• Students will understand what anxiety is and how it can affect them. • Students will identify common triggers of anxiety.
MATERIALS	• Definition of Anxiety Coloring Sheet (Middle/High) • Colored pencils, markers, or crayons

Introduction

- Begin the lesson by asking students to share if they have ever felt anxious or stressed and what those experiences were like.
- Stress that anxiety is a normal part of life that we will all experience.

    Often anxiety can be helpful. Anxiety can let us know that we care about something, and we might be worried that we will not do a good job. For example, you might get nervous and worried before you perform in front of an audience. You want to do well, and it is common to feel some anxiety because you are afraid you might forget the words or miss a note.

    Sometimes we feel anxiety because we feel like we are in danger and could get hurt. An example is when we hear a lot of thunder in a storm or even a tornado siren. We might feel some anxiety because we are afraid we could get hurt in a storm. The anxiety urges us to make sure that we are taking precautions to stay safe.

What Is Anxiety?

- Introduce the definition of anxiety:

    Anxiety is the excessive concern about a potential triggering event or perceived threat to one's safety. That safety can be physical, emotional, or social.

- Distribute the **Definition of Anxiety Coloring Sheet (Middle/High)** and the **colored pencils, markers, or crayons.**

- Anxiety comes from a fear or threat. Lead a discussion about the difference between a real, potential, or perceived threat. Explain that if a person believes that something could be a threat, it can cause anxiety.

- Next, discuss physical, emotional, and social safety. Ask students to suggest examples of each kind of threat. We are afraid of getting physically hurt, having our feelings hurt, or even having our friendships or reputations damaged. Remind them that what one student perceives as a threat does not have to be a threat to another person (and the other way around).

20

15-MINUTE FOCUS
Anxiety Workbook: Tips and Strategies to Manage Anxiety, Build Resilience, and Foster Emotional Well-Being

What Makes Us Anxious?

- Explain to the students about triggers.

  Our anxiety is caused by a trigger, an event that makes you feel anxious. It could be taking a test, going to a new school, joining a new team, being in a crowd, or storms. Triggers are warnings to your brain that the thing you are afraid of or feel threatened by is getting ready to happen. What is a trigger for one student may not be a trigger for another.

- Divide the class into small groups. Instruct the groups to brainstorm triggers that middle school students could encounter. Encourage them to consider things related to academics, friends, family, community, health, and social media.

- Allow the students to brainstorm for 7–8 minutes and then have each group share examples of triggers they identified.

Wrap Up & Assessment

- Ask students to repeat the definition of anxiety.
- Encourage students to watch for the triggers of anxiety they may encounter before the next class.

15-MINUTE FOCUS
Anxiety Workbook: Tips and Strategies to Manage Anxiety, Build Resilience, and Foster Emotional Well-Being

21

ANXIETY

ANXIETY IS THE EXCESSIVE CONCERN ABOUT A POTENTIAL TRIGGERING EVENT OR PERCEIVED THREAT TO ONE'S SAFETY. THAT SAFETY CAN BE PHYSICAL, EMOTIONAL, OR SOCIAL.

22

15-MINUTE FOCUS
Anxiety Workbook: Tips and Strategies to Manage Anxiety, Build Resilience, and Foster Emotional Well-Being

HIGH

LESSON LENGTH	40 minutes
OBJECTIVES	• Students will understand what anxiety is and how it can affect them. • Students will identify common triggers of anxiety.
MATERIALS	• Definition of Anxiety Coloring Sheet (Middle/High) • Colored pencils, markers, or crayons

 5 MINUTES

Introduction

- Begin the lesson by asking students to share when they have felt anxious or stressed and what those experiences were like.

  Stress that anxiety is a normal part of life that we will all experience. Often anxiety can be helpful. Anxiety can let us know that we care about something, and we might be worried that we will not do a good job. For example, you might get nervous and worried before you perform in front of an audience. You want to do well, and it is common to feel some anxiety because you are afraid you might forget the words or miss a note.

  Sometimes we feel anxiety because we feel like we are in danger and could get hurt. An example is when we hear a lot of thunder in a storm or even a tornado siren. We might feel some anxiety because we are afraid we could get hurt in a storm. The anxiety urges us to make sure that we are taking precautions to stay safe.

15-MINUTE FOCUS
Anxiety Workbook: Tips and Strategies to Manage Anxiety, Build Resilience, and Foster Emotional Well-Being

23

What Is Anxiety?

15 MINUTES

- Distribute the **Definition of Anxiety Coloring Sheet (Middle/High)** and the **colored pencils, markers, or crayons.**
- Introduce the definition of anxiety:

    Anxiety is the excessive concern about a potential triggering event or perceived threat to one's safety. That safety can be physical, emotional, or social.

    Anxiety comes from a fear or threat. Lead a discussion about the difference between a real, potential, or perceived threat. Explain that if a person believes that something could be a threat, it can cause anxiety.

- Next discuss physical, emotional, and social safety. Ask students to suggest examples of each kind of threat.

    We are afraid of getting physically hurt, having our feelings hurt, or even having our friendships or reputations damaged. What one student perceives as a threat does not have to be a threat to another person (and the other way around).

- Lead a discussion with students about the impact of anxiety on mental health and well-being. Suggested probing questions include:
    - How does anxiety impact how we feel about ourselves?
    - What happens if we do not learn strategies to manage and reduce anxiety?
    - Should we try to avoid all anxiety in our lives?
    - Anxiety can be very isolating. Why is it important to remember that everyone experiences anxiety?

What Makes Us Anxious?

15 MINUTES

- Explain to the students about triggers.

    Our anxiety is caused by a trigger, an event that makes you feel anxious. It could be taking a test, going to a new school, joining a new team, being in a crowd, or a storm. The triggers are warnings to your brain that the thing you are afraid of or feel threatened by is getting ready to happen. What is a trigger for one student may not be a trigger for another.

- Divide the class into small groups. Instruct the groups to brainstorm triggers that high school students encounter. Encourage them to consider things related to academics, friends, family, community, health, and social media.
- Allow the students to brainstorm for ten minutes and then have each group share examples of triggers they identified.

Wrap Up & Assessment

- Ask students to repeat the definition of anxiety.
- Encourage students to watch for the triggers of anxiety they may encounter before the next class.

15-MINUTE FOCUS
Anxiety Workbook: Tips and Strategies to Manage Anxiety, Build Resilience, and Foster Emotional Well-Being

25

What Anxiety Feels Like

ELEMENTARY

LESSON LENGTH	25 minutes
OBJECTIVES	• Students will identify physical, emotional, and behavioral symptoms of anxiety. • Students will connect symptoms of anxiety to triggers of anxiety.
MATERIALS	• How Anxiety Feels in My Body Worksheet • Colored pencils, markers, or crayons

5 MINUTES

Introduction

- Remind the students that anxiety is our body's response to a fear or threat to our physical, emotional, or social safety. Ask students to echo *"Anxiety is worry and fear."*
- Explain that in the previous lesson, we discussed what anxiety is and some of the triggers that cause anxiety.

15 MINUTES

How Anxiety Feels in My Body

- Share about how our bodies show we are anxious.

  Sometimes it is hard to know what is causing our anxiety. When that happens, our bodies can give us clues. These clues are called symptoms of anxiety. We can have physical, emotional, and behavioral symptoms of anxiety.

- Share examples of **physical symptoms** of anxiety such as: increased heart rate, tense muscles, increased blood pressure, excessive sweating, rapid breathing, headaches, nausea, digestive issues, poor sleep, feeling jittery or lightheaded, a hot face, clammy hands, or dry mouth.

- Share examples of **emotional symptoms**. These often include feeling afraid, worried, or nervous; constant worries or concerns about family, school, friends, or activities; repetitive, unwanted thoughts or actions, fears of embarrassment or making mistakes, low self-esteem, lack of self-confidence, or crying.

26

15-MINUTE FOCUS
Anxiety Workbook: Tips and Strategies to Manage Anxiety, Build Resilience, and Foster Emotional Well-Being

- Share **behavioral symptoms**. These often include refusing to talk; clinging to caregivers, siblings, or trusted adults; acting scared or upset, startling easily, missing school, refusing to do things, avoiding people, or having tantrums.
- Distribute the **How Anxiety Feels in My Body Worksheet** and **colored pencils, markers, or crayons** to students. They can color it as time allows.
- The student will identify where they feel anxiety in their body. Students should write anxiety symptoms they experience in the bubbles, then draw lines from each bubble to where they feel each symptom in their body. For emotional symptoms such as sadness, they could draw a line to their heart. For behavioral symptoms such as running away, they can draw a line to their feet. It is okay for students to draw more than one line to the same area of the body. Once all students have had time to identify their personal anxiety symptoms, discuss what symptoms they have in common and which ones are different.

Wrap Up & Assessment

- Ask the students what symptoms of anxiety tell us.

15-MINUTE FOCUS
Anxiety Workbook: Tips and Strategies to Manage Anxiety, Build Resilience, and Foster Emotional Well-Being

27

How Anxiety Feels in My Body

Color the student below to reflect you. Where do you feel anxiety in your body?
Write those symptoms in the bubbles on the sides and draw lines to
the part of your body where you feel anxious.

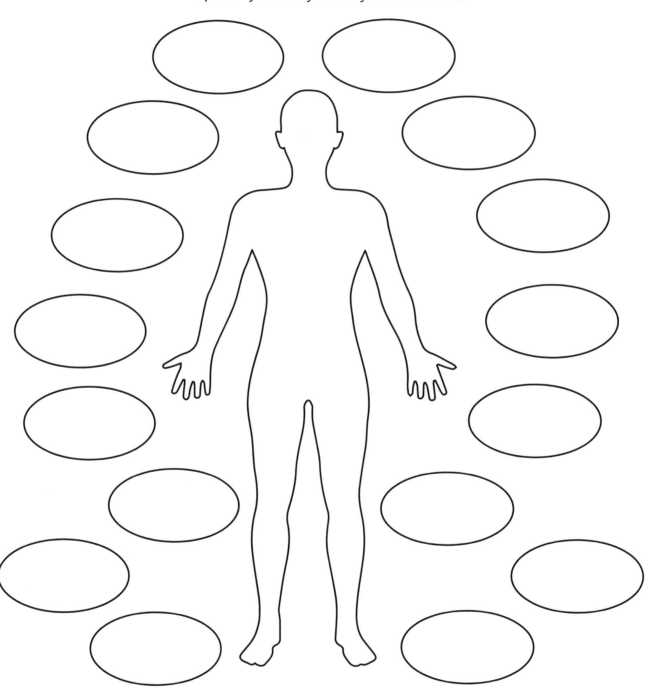

Word bank:

Heart beats fast
Muscles get tight
Lots of sweating
Breathing fast

Head hurts
Tummy gets upset
Not sleeping well
Feeling shaky

Feeling dizzy
Face turns red or feels hot
Hands feel sweaty
Mouth gets dry

MIDDLE

LESSON LENGTH	40 minutes
OBJECTIVES	• Students will identify physical, emotional, and behavioral symptoms of anxiety. • Students will connect symptoms of anxiety to triggers of anxiety.
MATERIALS	• How Anxiety Feels in My Body Worksheet • Colored pencils, markers, or crayons

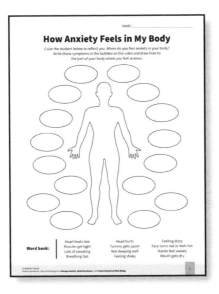

Introduction

5 MINUTES

• Ask students to recall the definition of anxiety:

Anxiety is the excessive concern about a potential triggering event or perceived threat to one's safety. That safety can be physical, emotional, or social.

• Remind them that in the previous lesson we discussed what anxiety is and some of the triggers that cause anxiety. Allow students to share if they noticed any triggers of anxiety since the last lesson.

Symptoms of Anxiety

10 MINUTES

• Share about how our bodies show we are anxious.

Sometimes it is hard to know what is causing our anxiety. When that happens, our bodies can give us clues. These clues are called symptoms of anxiety. We can have physical, emotional, and behavioral symptoms of anxiety.

15-MINUTE FOCUS
Anxiety Workbook: Tips and Strategies to Manage Anxiety, Build Resilience, and Foster Emotional Well-Being

29

- Share examples of **physical symptoms** of anxiety such as: increased heart rate, tense muscles, increased blood pressure, excessive sweating, rapid breathing, headaches, nausea, digestive issues, poor sleep, feeling jittery or lightheaded, a hot face, clammy hands, or dry mouth.

- Share examples of **emotional symptoms**, which often include feeling afraid, worried, or nervous; constant worries or concerns about family, school, friends, or activities; repetitive, unwanted thoughts or actions, fears of embarrassment or making mistakes, low self-esteem, lack of self-confidence, crying.

- Share **behavioral symptoms**, which often include refusing to talk; clinging to caregivers, siblings, or trusted adults; acting scared or upset, startling easily, missing school, refusing to do things, avoiding people, having tantrums.

- Allow students to suggest additional symptoms they may have experienced.

How Anxiety Feels in My Body

- Distribute the **How Anxiety Feels in My Body Worksheet** and **colored pencils, markers, or crayons** to students. They can color it as time allows.

- The student will identify where they feel anxiety in their body. Students should write anxiety symptoms they experience in the bubbles, then draw lines from each bubble to where they feel each symptom in their body.

- Suggest that they circle the heart if they have strong feelings. If they have negative thoughts, they might circle their brain. If they get sweaty palms, they might draw sweat on their hands and then circle them. They may also list their symptoms and draw lines to the areas of their bodies where the symptoms occur.

- Once students have had time to identify their personal anxiety symptoms, instruct them to turn to a neighbor and discuss what symptoms they have in common and which ones are different.

- Facilitate a class discussion once the pairs have shared together. Consider the following questions for discussion:

    What did you learn about your own anxiety? What symptoms did you have in common with your partner? Did anyone have exactly the same symptoms as their partner? How can knowing our symptoms of anxiety help us to identify our anxiety triggers?

    Symptoms can alert us that a triggering event is happening. When we notice the symptoms, we can pay attention to what is happening around us. This helps us to learn what is causing our anxiety.

Wrap Up & Assessment

Ask students to write down any triggers that came to mind when they were thinking about their symptoms of anxiety. Remind them that the symptoms of anxiety are the body's warning system so we should pay attention.

30

15-MINUTE FOCUS
Anxiety Workbook: Tips and Strategies to Manage Anxiety, Build Resilience, and Foster Emotional Well-Being

HIGH

LESSON LENGTH	40 minutes
OBJECTIVES	• Students will identify physical, emotional, and behavioral symptoms of anxiety. • Students will connect symptoms of anxiety to triggers of anxiety.
MATERIALS	• How Anxiety Feels in My Body Worksheet • Colored pencils, markers, or crayons

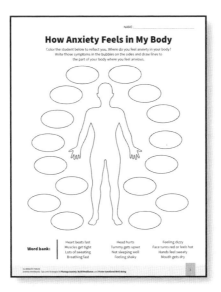

5 MINUTES — Introduction

- Ask students to recall the definition of anxiety:

  Anxiety is the excessive concern about a potential triggering event or perceived threat to one's safety. That safety can be physical, emotional, or social.

- Remind them that in the previous lesson we discussed what anxiety is and some of the triggers that cause anxiety. Allow students to share if they noticed any triggers of anxiety since the last lesson.

10 MINUTES — Symptoms of Anxiety

- Share about how our bodies show we are anxious.

  Sometimes it is hard to know what is causing our anxiety. When that happens, our bodies can give us clues. These clues are called symptoms of anxiety. We can have physical, emotional, and behavioral symptoms of anxiety.

15-MINUTE FOCUS
Anxiety Workbook: Tips and Strategies to Manage Anxiety, Build Resilience, and Foster Emotional Well-Being

31

- Share examples of **physical symptoms** of anxiety such as: increased heart rate, tense muscles, increased blood pressure, excessive sweating, rapid breathing, headaches, nausea, digestive issues, poor sleep, feeling jittery or lightheaded, a hot face, clammy hands, or dry mouth.
- Share examples of **emotional symptoms**, which often include feeling afraid, worried, or nervous; constant worries or concerns about family, school, friends, or activities; repetitive, unwanted thoughts or actions, fears of embarrassment or making mistakes, low self-esteem, lack of self-confidence, crying.
- Share **behavioral symptoms**, which often include refusing to talk; clinging to caregivers, siblings, or trusted adults; acting scared or upset, startling easily, missing school, refusing to do things, avoiding people, having tantrums.
- Allow students to suggest additional symptoms they may have experienced.

How Anxiety Feels in My Body

- Distribute the **How Anxiety Feels in My Body Worksheet** and **colored pencils, markers, or crayons** to students. They can color it as time allows.
- The student will identify where they feel anxiety in their body. Students should write anxiety symptoms they experience in the bubbles, then draw lines from each bubble to where they feel each symptom in their body.
- Suggest that they circle the heart if they have strong feelings. If they have negative thoughts, they might circle their brain. If they get sweaty palms, they might draw sweat on their hands and then circle them. They may also list their symptoms and draw lines to the areas of their bodies where the symptoms occur.
- Once students have had time to identify their personal anxiety symptoms, instruct them to turn to a neighbor and discuss what symptoms they have in common and which ones are different.
- Facilitate a class discussion once the pairs have shared together. Consider the following questions for discussion:

  What did you learn about your own anxiety? What symptoms did you have in common with your partner? Did anyone have exactly the same symptoms as their partner? How can knowing our symptoms of anxiety help us to identify our anxiety triggers?

  Symptoms can alert us that a triggering event is happening. When we notice the symptoms, we can pay attention to what is happening around us. This helps us to learn what is causing our anxiety.

Wrap Up & Assessment

Ask students to write down any trigger that came to mind when they were thinking about their symptoms of anxiety. Remind them that the symptoms of anxiety are the body's warning system so we should pay attention.

Fight, Flight, Freeze, Fawn Response

ELEMENTARY

LESSON LENGTH	25 minutes
OBJECTIVES	• Students will identify the three parts of the brain that are involved in the anxiety response. • Students will describe the Fight, Flight, Freeze, Fawn response to anxiety.
MATERIALS	• Anxiety Starts in Our Brain Worksheet • Fight, Flight, Freeze, Fawn Response Handout • What Does Fight, Flight, Freeze, and Fawn Look Like? Handout

3 MINUTES

Introduction

- Begin the lesson by briefly reviewing the concepts of anxiety, triggers, and symptoms from the previous lessons. Ask students if they have noticed any symptoms of anxiety.

- Explain that we sometimes experience intense feelings of anxiety. These usually come on quickly and we may or may not be able to identify the trigger. We show a lot of symptoms such as fast heartbeat, shallow breathing, sweating, headache, and dizziness.

15-MINUTE FOCUS
Anxiety Workbook: Tips and Strategies to Manage Anxiety, Build Resilience, and Foster Emotional Well-Being

33

Anxiety Starts in Our Brain

10
MINUTES

- Distribute the **Anxiety Starts in Our Brain Worksheet** to students. Review the three different parts of the brain with the students.

  *The **cerebrum** is the thinking brain. It controls cognitive and executive functions, and the ability to evaluate a situation. The **amygdala** is the feeling brain. It controls your emotions. The survival brain is the **brain stem**, which controls the systems that keep us alive such as breathing, blood pumping, reflexes, and digestion. These are called **autonomic systems** because they happen automatically. How many of you have to tell your lungs to breathe or your heart to pump blood throughout your body? We don't. Our brain stem sends messages to keep those systems going.*

- Explain how when the brain notices a trigger it must determine whether there is a threat. Ask the students if they can guess which part of the brain will determine if something is a threat. The thinking brain (cerebrum) usually makes that decision.

  *If the **trigger** is something new, associated with a negative experience, or something we know can hurt us physically, hurt our feelings, or hurt our relationships, our amygdala will step in and take over.*

  What does the amygdala control in the brain? (Feelings.)

  *When the amygdala takes over, it sends messages to the thinking part of the brain to shut down, like turning off a computer. The amygdala is focused on **avoiding getting hurt**. It does not want to spend any time thinking about the situation. It wants to act.*

  After it shuts off the thinking brain, the amygdala sends a message to the survival brain (the brain stem) that it needs to do something to protect the body. The survival brain will then send messages to tell those systems to get going. That is why we start to feel our heartbeat faster, why we breathe short quick breaths, and why we sometimes get stomachaches when we feel anxiety. Our brain stem is directing our body to move us to safety.

- Ask the students to complete the worksheet, labeling the parts of the brain on the space provided.

- Allow students to ask questions to assess for understanding.

10
MINUTES

Fight, Flight, Freeze, Fawn Response

- Explain that when our brain stem sends a message to our systems to seek safety there are four different responses that we typically take. Distribute the **Fight, Flight, Freeze, Fawn Response Handout** and the **What Does Fight, Flight, Freeze, and Fawn Look Like? Handout**.

- You can explain each response, highlighting each one and noting what actions our bodies might take. Allow the students to act out the physical response (pretending to fight, of course).

    Fight means to face the danger and fight the threat aggressively.

    Flight means to run away from the threat to try and save yourself.

    Freeze means to not move or to hide in hopes of being ignored until the threat passes.

    Fawn means to submit to or to bargain with the threat in hopes of avoiding conflict.

- There are also many videos to help explain the Fight, Flight, Freeze, Fawn response. The Fawn response is a relatively new addition to the response and some videos have not addressed it. Be prepared to add an explanation about it after a video. Here is an option for Elementary students.

    - "Fight Flight Freeze – A Guide to Anxiety for Kids" (Anxiety Canada) https://www.youtube.com/watch?v=FfSbWc3O_5M

2
MINUTES

Wrap Up & Assessment

- Ask students to explain one way the Fight, Flight, Freeze, Fawn response helps protect them in challenging situations.

- Challenge the students to notice if they experience the Fight, Flight, Freeze, Fawn response this week.

15-MINUTE FOCUS
Anxiety Workbook: Tips and Strategies to Manage Anxiety, Build Resilience, and Foster Emotional Well-Being

35

NAME:_____

Anxiety Starts in Our Brain

Label the Feeling Brain, Survival Brain, and Thinking Brain.

_____

CEREBRUM

_____

AMYGDALA

_____

BRAIN STEM

FIGHT, FLIGHT, FREEZE, OR FAWN RESPONSE

15-MINUTE FOCUS
Anxiety Workbook: Tips and Strategies to Manage Anxiety, Build Resilience, and Foster Emotional Well-Being

37

What Does Fight, Flight, Freeze, and Fawn Look Like?

Fight can look like:

- kicking
- screaming
- spitting
- pushing
- throwing anything he can get his hands on
- his hands clasped in fists, ready to punch
- glaring
- clawing at the air
- gasping for breath

Flight can look like:

- darting eyes
- restlessness
- excessive fidgeting
- doing anything to get away
- running without concern for his own safety

Freeze can look like:

- holding his breath
- heart pounding and/or decreased heart rate
- shutting down
- feeling unable to move
- escaping into his own mind
- feeling numb
- whining
- daydreaming

Fawn can look like:

- bargaining
- giving in
- people-pleasing
- lacking boundaries
- having no personal preferences
- deferring to the source of threat

38

15-MINUTE FOCUS
Anxiety Workbook: Tips and Strategies to Manage Anxiety, Build Resilience, and Foster Emotional Well-Being

MIDDLE

LESSON LENGTH	25 minutes
OBJECTIVES	• Students will identify the three parts of the brain that are involved in the anxiety response. • Students will describe the Fight, Flight, Freeze, Fawn response to anxiety.
MATERIALS	• Anxiety Starts in Our Brain Worksheet • Fight, Flight, Freeze, Fawn Response Handout • What Does Fight, Flight, Freeze, and Fawn Look Like? Handout

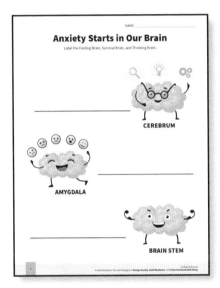

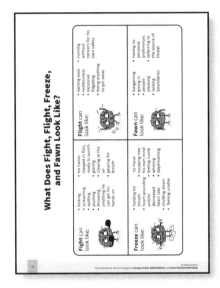

3 MINUTES

Introduction

- Begin the lesson by briefly reviewing the concepts of anxiety, triggers, and symptoms from the previous lessons. Ask students if they have noticed any symptoms of anxiety.

- Explain that sometimes we experience intense feelings of anxiety. These usually come on quickly and we may or may not be able to identify the trigger. We show a lot of symptoms such as fast heartbeat, shallow breathing, sweating, headache, and dizziness.

15-MINUTE FOCUS
Anxiety Workbook: Tips and Strategies to Manage Anxiety, Build Resilience, and Foster Emotional Well-Being

39

Anxiety Starts in Our Brain

- Distribute the **Anxiety Starts in Our Brain Worksheet** to students. Review the three different parts of the brain with the students.

    *The **cerebrum** is the thinking brain. It controls all cognitive and executive functions, as well as the ability to evaluate a situation. The **amygdala** is the feeling brain. It controls your emotions. The survival brain is the **brain stem**, which controls the body's systems that keep us alive such as breathing, blood pumping, reflexes, and digestion. These are called **autonomic systems** because they happen automatically. How many of you have to tell your lungs to breathe or your heart to pump blood throughout your body? We don't. Our brain stem sends messages to keep those systems going.*

- Explain how when the brain notices a trigger it must determine whether it is a threat. Ask the students if they can guess which part of the brain will determine if something is a threat. The thinking brain (cerebrum) usually makes that decision.

    *But if the **trigger** is something new, associated with a negative experience, or something we know can hurt us physically, hurt our feelings, or hurt our relationships, our amygdala will step in and take over.*

    What does the amygdala control in the brain? (Feelings.)

    *When the amygdala takes over, it sends messages to the thinking part of the brain to shut down, like turning off a computer. It is focused on **avoiding getting hurt**. The amygdala does not want to spend any time thinking about the situation. It wants to act.*

    After it shuts off the thinking brain, the amygdala sends a message to the survival brain (the brain stem) that it needs to do something to protect the body. The survival brain will then send messages to tell those systems to get going. That is why we start to feel our hearts beat faster, why we breathe short quick breaths, and why we sometimes get stomachaches when we feel anxiety. Our brain stem is directing our body to move us to safety.

- Allow students to ask questions to assess for understanding.
- Ask the students to complete the worksheet, labeling the parts of the brain on the space provided.

40

15-MINUTE FOCUS
Anxiety Workbook: Tips and Strategies to Manage Anxiety, Build Resilience, and Foster Emotional Well-Being

Fight, Flight, Freeze, Fawn Response

- Explain that when our brain stem sends a message to our systems to seek safety there are four different responses that we typically take. Distribute the **Fight, Flight, Freeze, Fawn Response Handout** and the **What Does Fight, Flight, Freeze, and Fawn Look Like? Handout**.

- You can explain each response, highlighting each response and what actions our bodies might take.

  Fight means to face the danger and fight the threat aggressively.

  Flight means to run away from the threat to try and save yourself.

  Freeze means to not move or to hide in hopes of being ignored until the threat passes.

  Fawn means to submit to or to bargain with the threat in hopes of avoiding conflict.

- Suggest that students relate each response to animals' reactions to threats.

  Imagine that a tiger likely fights when a threat approaches. A rabbit often runs away to seek shelter when a threat approaches. A chameleon freezes and changes color to blend into the environment in hopes of not being seen by the threat. A puppy may try to cuddle with a cat who is trying to assert its dominance in the family home. These responses are instincts that are designed to keep us safe.

- There are also many videos to help explain the Fight, Flight, Freeze, Fawn response. The Fawn response is a relatively new addition to the responses and some videos have not addressed it. Be prepared to add an explanation about it after a video. Here are some possible videos:

  - "Exploring Anxiety and Stress Management (Teens)" (Kids Helpline) https://www.youtube.com/watch?v=GQSfW4xrKSk

  - "Fight Flight Freeze – Anxiety Explained For Teens" (Anxiety Canada) https://www.youtube.com/watch?v=rpolpKTWrp4

- After explaining the Fight, Flight, Freeze, Fawn response, ask students how each of the responses can keep them safe in some of the situations that trigger the anxieties they discussed in the previous lesson.

Wrap Up & Assessment

- Ask students to explain one way the Fight, Flight, Freeze, Fawn response helps protect them in challenging situations.
- Challenge the students to notice if they experience the Fight, Flight, Freeze, Fawn response during the coming week.

15-MINUTE FOCUS
Anxiety Workbook: Tips and Strategies to Manage Anxiety, Build Resilience, and Foster Emotional Well-Being

41

HIGH

LESSON LENGTH	40 minutes
OBJECTIVES	• Students will identify the three parts of the brain that are involved in the anxiety response. • Students will describe the Fight, Flight, Freeze, Fawn response to anxiety.
MATERIALS	• Anxiety Starts in Our Brain Worksheet • Fight, Flight, Freeze, Fawn Response Handout • What Does Fight, Flight, Freeze, and Fawn Look Like? Handout

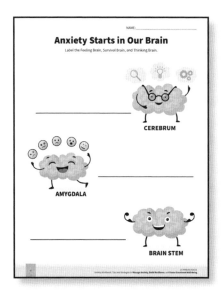

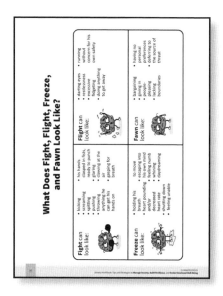

3 MINUTES Introduction

- Begin the lesson by briefly reviewing the concepts of anxiety, triggers, and symptoms from the previous lessons. Ask students if they have noticed any symptoms of anxiety.

- Explain that sometimes we experience intense feelings of anxiety. These usually come on quickly and we may or may not be able to identify the trigger. We show a lot of symptoms such as fast heartbeat, shallow breathing, sweating, headache, and dizziness.

Anxiety Starts in Our Brain

10 MINUTES

- Distribute the **Anxiety Starts in Our Brain Worksheet** to students. Review the three different parts of the brain with the students.

  *The **cerebrum** is the thinking brain. It controls all cognitive and executive functions, as well as the ability to evaluate a situation. The **amygdala** is the feeling brain. It controls your emotions. The survival brain is the **brain stem**, which controls the body's systems that keep us alive such as breathing, blood pumping, reflexes, and digestion. These are called **autonomic systems** because they happen automatically. How many of you have to tell your lungs to breathe or your heart to pump blood throughout your body? We don't. Our brain stem sends messages to keep those systems going.*

- Explain how when the brain notices a trigger it must determine whether it is a threat. Ask the students if they can guess which part of the brain will determine if something is a threat. The thinking brain (cerebrum) usually makes that decision.

  *But if the **trigger** is something new, associated with a negative experience, or something we know can hurt us physically, hurt our feelings, or hurt our relationships, our amygdala will step in and take over.*

  What does the amygdala control in the brain? (Feelings.)

  *When the amygdala takes over, it sends messages to the thinking part of the brain to shut down, like turning off a computer. It is focused on **avoiding getting hurt**. The amygdala does not want to spend any time thinking about the situation. It wants to act.*

  After it shuts off the thinking brain, the amygdala sends a message to the survival brain (the brain stem) that it needs to do something to protect the body. The survival brain will then send messages to tell those systems to get going. That is why we start to feel our hearts beat faster, why we breathe short quick breaths, and why we sometimes get stomachaches when we feel anxiety. Our brain stem is directing our body to move us to safety.

- Allow students to ask questions to assess for understanding.
- Ask the students to complete the worksheet, labeling the parts of the brain on the space provided.

15-MINUTE FOCUS
Anxiety Workbook: Tips and Strategies to Manage Anxiety, Build Resilience, and Foster Emotional Well-Being

43

Fight, Flight, Freeze, Fawn Response

- Explain that when our brain stem sends a message to our systems to seek safety there are four different responses that we typically take. Distribute the **Fight, Flight, Freeze, Fawn Response Handout** and the **What Does Fight, Flight, Freeze, and Fawn Look Like? Handout**.

- You can explain each response, highlighting each response and what actions our bodies might take.

  Fight means to face the danger and fight the threat aggressively.

  Flight means to run away from the threat to try and save yourself.

  Freeze means to not move or to hide in hopes of being ignored until the threat passes.

  Fawn means to submit to or to bargain with the threat in hopes of avoiding conflict.

- Suggest that students relate each response to animals' reactions to threats.

  Imagine that a tiger likely fights when a threat approaches. A rabbit often runs away to seek shelter when a threat approaches. A chameleon freezes and changes color to blend into the environment in hopes of not being seen by the threat. A puppy may try to cuddle with a cat who is trying to assert its dominance in the family home. These responses are instincts that are designed to keep us safe.

- There are also many videos to help explain the Fight, Flight, Freeze, Fawn response. The Fawn response is a relatively new addition to the responses and some videos have not addressed it. Be prepared to add an explanation about it after a video. Here are some possible videos:

  - "Exploring Anxiety and Stress Management (Teens)" (Kids Helpline) https://www.youtube.com/watch?v=GQSfW4xrKSk

  - "Fight Flight Freeze – Anxiety Explained For Teens" (Anxiety Canada) https://www.youtube.com/watch?v=rpolpKTWrp4

- After explaining the Fight, Flight, Freeze, Fawn response, ask students how each of the responses can keep them safe in some of the situations that trigger the anxieties they discussed in the previous lesson.

44

15-MINUTE FOCUS
Anxiety Workbook: Tips and Strategies to Manage Anxiety, Build Resilience, and Foster Emotional Well-Being

Applying Fight, Flight, Freeze, Fawn Response

- Divide the class into groups. Instruct them to identify an anxiety-triggering event.
- Have each group identify what each of the responses might look like in that situation.

  For example, if the trigger is speaking in front of a class, what might the fight response look like? The flight response? Freeze response? And the fawn response?

- Once groups have identified their responses, allow them to share their triggers and responses with the class.

Wrap Up & Assessment

- Ask students to explain one way the Fight, Flight, Freeze, Fawn response helps protect them in challenging situations.
- Challenge the students to notice if they experience the Fight, Flight, Freeze, Fawn response during the coming week.

15-MINUTE FOCUS
Anxiety Workbook: Tips and Strategies to Manage Anxiety, Build Resilience, and Foster Emotional Well-Being

45

Coping Strategies for Managing Anxiety

ELEMENTARY

LESSON LENGTH	25 minutes
OBJECTIVES	• Students will explain how coping strategies help manage anxiety. • Students will identify 2–3 coping strategies they will practice managing their anxiety.
MATERIALS	• Coping Skills for Kids Coloring Sheet • Coping Skills Picture List Handout • Colored pencils, markers, or crayons

5 MINUTES

Introduction

- Review the parts of the brain involved in anxiety and the Fight, Flight, Freeze, Fawn response discussed in the previous lesson.
- Allow a few students to share when they noticed using the Fight, Flight, Freeze, Fawn response during the past week. Help them identify the triggering event, their response, and how the response kept them safe.

5 MINUTES

Managing Anxiety

- Share that everyone has tools they can use to help manage and reduce their anxiety. We call those tools coping skills. Ask students if they know of any coping skills. Focus on appropriate coping skills. If a student suggests an inappropriate coping skill, use it as an opportunity to reinforce that we want to use tools that will help us.

  Doing something that could get us in trouble, even if it reduces our anxiety in the moment, will likely result in more anxiety and problems in the future.

  Coping skills *should:*

  – *Remind our brains that we are safe.*

  – *Slow our breathing down to let our thinking brain re-engage.*

  – *Distract our amygdala by giving it another feeling to process.*

  – *Use the energy our survival brain is generating in a more productive way.*

46

15-MINUTE FOCUS
Anxiety Workbook: Tips and Strategies to Manage Anxiety, Build Resilience, and Foster Emotional Well-Being

Identify and Practice Coping Skills

10 MINUTES

- Choose from one of the following activities that encourage students to identify and practice various coping skills.
  - **Activity 1:** Distribute the **Coping Skills for Kids Coloring Sheet** and the **colored pencils, markers, or crayons.** Have the students color the worksheet as you discuss the coping skills listed, making sure to explain any that are unfamiliar to students. If students indicate they have used any of the skills before, allow them to share how the skill helped them feel.

  - **Activity 2:** Distribute the **Coping Skills Picture List Handout**. Review the coping skills listed, making sure to explain any that are unfamiliar to students. In a fun twist on charades, have one student choose a coping skill from the sheet and act it out without speaking while the rest of the class guesses which strategy is being demonstrated. Rotate and let different students take turns acting out coping strategies.

Wrap Up & Assessment

5 MINUTES

- Ask students to circle 2-3 coping skills on the worksheet they will use when feeling anxious.
- Summarize the key points learned during the lessons about anxiety.
- Encourage students to remember that it is okay to feel anxious sometimes and that there are effective ways to cope with those feelings. If they need to talk more about their experiences with anxiety, remind them of the school staff there to support them (teacher, school counselor, school social worker, etc.) as well as their caregiver.

Note: Throughout the curriculum, be mindful of students who might be experiencing anxiety themselves. Create a supportive and safe environment for sharing and learning. If any student is consistently exhibiting signs of severe anxiety or distress, it is essential to involve school counselors or other appropriate personnel to provide additional support.

15-MINUTE FOCUS
Anxiety Workbook: Tips and Strategies to Manage Anxiety, Build Resilience, and Foster Emotional Well-Being

47

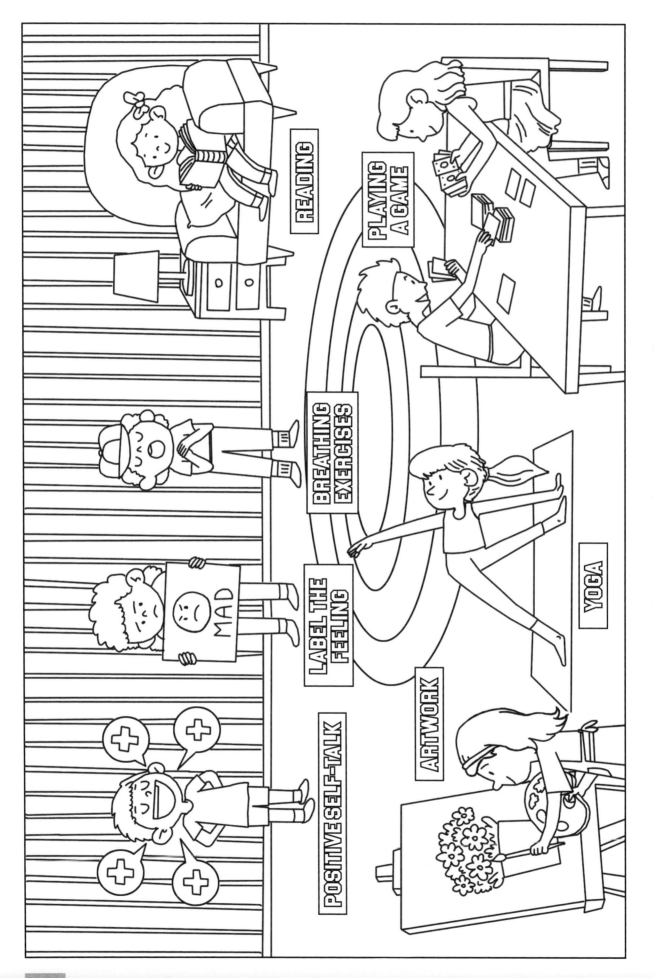

Coping Skills for Kids

Coping Skills

 MEDITATE

 EXERCISE

 WRITE IN JOURNAL

 DRAW

 LISTEN TO MUSIC

 TAKE A BATH

 PLAY WITH PET

 ENJOY NATURE

 CLEAN THE HOUSE

 READ A BOOK

 USE AROMATHERAPY

 PLAY A GAME

 COOK A MEAL

 KNITTING

 PRAY

 FINDING HUMOR

 MAKE A GRATITUDE LIST

 COLORING

 GARDENING

 DO YOGA

 GET ENOUGH SLEEP

 ACCEPT A CHALLENGE

 DRINK TEA

 SQUEEZE A STRESS BALL

 PLAY MUSICAL INSTRUMENT

 ASK FOR HELP

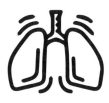 PRACTICE DEEP/ SLOW BREATHING

 EAT HEALTHY FOOD

 LIMIT CAFFEINE

 SCHEDULE TIME FOR YOURSELF

 CRY

 SMILE

 TAKE A WALK

 DOODLE ON PAPER

 GO SEE A MOVIE

 EAT A LITTLE CHOCOLATE

15-MINUTE FOCUS
Anxiety Workbook: Tips and Strategies to Manage Anxiety, Build Resilience, and Foster Emotional Well-Being

49

MIDDLE

LESSON LENGTH	40 minutes
OBJECTIVES	• Students will explain how coping strategies help manage anxiety. • Students will identify 2–3 coping strategies they will practice managing their anxiety.
MATERIALS	• 50 Coping Skills Handout • Coping Skills Alphabet Handout • Coping Skills Alphabet Worksheet (Make Your Own)

Introduction

5 MINUTES

- Review the parts of the brain involved in anxiety and the Fight, Flight, Freeze, Fawn response discussed in the previous lesson.
- Allow a few students to share if they noticed using the Fight, Flight, Freeze, Fawn response during the past week. Help them identify the triggering event, their response, and how the response kept them safe.

Managing Anxiety

5 MINUTES

- Share that everyone has tools they can use to help manage and reduce their anxiety. We call those tools coping skills. Ask students if they know of any coping skills. Focus on appropriate coping skills. If a student suggests an inappropriate coping skill, use it as an opportunity to reinforce that we want to use tools that will help us.

  Doing something that could get us in trouble, even if it reduces our anxiety in the moment, will likely result in more anxiety and problems in the future.

  Coping skills *should:*

  – *Remind our brains that we are safe.*

  – *Slow our breathing down to let our thinking brain re-engage.*

  – *Distract our amygdala by giving it another feeling to process.*

  – *Use the energy our survival brain is generating in a more productive way.*

Identify and Practice Coping Skills

25 MINUTES

- Distribute either the **50 Coping Skills Handout** or the **Alphabet Coping Skills Handout**. Choose from one of the following activities that encourage students to identify and practice various coping skills.
    - **Activity 1:** Review the coping skills listed, making sure to explain any that are unfamiliar to students. As time allows, have the students demonstrate a couple of the coping skills. If students indicate they have used any of the skills before, allow them to share how the skill helped them feel.

    - **Activity 2:** Review the coping skills listed, making sure to explain any that are unfamiliar to students. In a fun twist on charades, have one student choose a coping skill from the sheet and act it out without speaking while the rest of the class guesses which strategy is being demonstrated. Rotate and let different students take turns acting out coping strategies.

    - **Bonus Activity:** Once students understand appropriate coping skills, using the **Alphabet Coping Skills Worksheet (Make Your Own)**, have them identify a coping skill they would use that starts with each letter of the alphabet. Encourage them to be creative. A variation of this activity is to instruct them to identify five coping skills that start with the same letter as their name.

Wrap Up & Assessment

5 MINUTES

- Ask students to circle 2-3 coping skills on the worksheet they will use when feeling anxious.
- Summarize the key points learned during the lessons about anxiety.
- Encourage students to remember that it is okay to feel anxious sometimes and that there are effective ways to cope with those feelings. If they need to talk more about their experiences with anxiety, remind them of the school staff there to support them (teacher, school counselor, school social worker, etc.) as well as their caregiver.

Note: Throughout the curriculum, be mindful of students who might be experiencing anxiety themselves. Create a supportive and safe environment for sharing and learning. If any student is consistently exhibiting signs of severe anxiety or distress, it is essential to involve school counselors or other appropriate personnel to provide additional support.

15-MINUTE FOCUS
Anxiety Workbook: Tips and Strategies to Manage Anxiety, Build Resilience, and Foster Emotional Well-Being

51

50 COPING SKILLS

1. Take Deep Breaths
2. Color a Picture
3. Squeeze a Stress Ball
4. Punch a Pillow
5. Blow Bubbles
6. Read a Book
7. Eat a Healthy Snack
8. Listen to Music
9. Play Outside
10. Talk to an Adult
11. Sing
12. Count to 10
13. Draw a Picture
14. Play a Board Game
15. Walk Away
16. Paint a Picture
17. Rip Paper
18. Play a Video Game
19. Go for a Walk
20. Write in a Journal
21. Talk to a Friend
22. Take a Nap
23. Hug a Stuffed Animal
24. Dance
25. Play with Play-Doh®
26. Put Together a Puzzle
27. Play an Instrument
28. Stretch
29. Play a Sport
30. Drink Cold Water
31. Give Someone a Hug
32. Build with Blocks
33. Play with Legos
34. Do Yoga
35. Exercise
36. Paint Your Nails
37. Take a Bubble Bath
38. Think of Something Funny
39. Take Pictures
40. Close Your Eyes
41. Use a Fidget Spinner
42. Chew Gum
43. Look at Old Pictures
44. Do Something Kind
45. Go for a Run
46. Do a Craft
47. Clean
48. Pet an Animal
49. Watch a Funny Video
50. Bake

Coping Skills Alphabet

A — Ask for Help

B — Belly Breathe

C — Count to 10

D — Draw a Picture

E — Exercise

F — Fidget Toy

G — Show Gratitude

H — Hug a Loved One

I — Imagine Your Safe Place

J — Journal

K — Show Kindness

L — Laugh

M — Mindfulness

N — Nap

O — Go Outside

P — Paint

Q — Find an Inspirational Quote

R — Read a Book

S — Squeeze a Stress Ball

T — Talk to Someone

U — Use Positive Self-Talk

V — Take a Mental Vacation

W — Drink Water

X — X-ray Your Feelings

Y — Yoga

Z — Zone Out to Music

15-MINUTE FOCUS
Anxiety Workbook: Tips and Strategies to Manage Anxiety, Build Resilience, and Foster Emotional Well-Being

53

Coping Skills Alphabet

In the box for each letter, write an activity you could do to help when you feel anxious.

HIGH

LESSON LENGTH	40 minutes
OBJECTIVES	• Students will explain how coping strategies help manage anxiety. • Students will identify 2–3 coping strategies they will practice managing their anxiety.
MATERIALS	• 50 Coping Skills Handout • Coping Skills Alphabet Handout • Coping Skills Alphabet Worksheet (Make Your Own) • My Anxiety Coping Skills Worksheet

Introduction

5 MINUTES

- Review the parts of the brain involved in anxiety and the Fight, Flight, Freeze, Fawn response discussed in the previous lesson.

- Allow a few students to share when they noticed using the Fight, Flight, Freeze, Fawn response during the past week. Help them identify the triggering event, their response, and how the response kept them safe.

15-MINUTE FOCUS
Anxiety Workbook: Tips and Strategies to Manage Anxiety, Build Resilience, and Foster Emotional Well-Being

55

5 MINUTES

Managing Anxiety

- Share that everyone has tools they can use to help manage and reduce their anxiety. We call those tools coping skills. Ask students if they know of any coping skills. Focus on appropriate coping skills. If a student suggests an inappropriate coping skill, use it as an opportunity to reinforce that we want to use tools that will help us.

    Doing something that could get us in trouble, even if it reduces our anxiety in the moment, will likely result in more anxiety and problems in the future.

    Coping skills *should:*

    - *Remind our brains that we are safe.*
    - *Slow our breathing down to let our thinking brain re-engage.*
    - *Distract our amygdala by giving it another feeling to process.*
    - *Use the energy our survival brain is generating in a more productive way.*

25 MINUTES

Identify and Practice Coping Skills

- Distribute either the **50 Coping Skills Handout** or the **Alphabet Coping Skills Handout**. Choose from one of the following activities that encourage students to identify and practice various coping skills.

    - **Activity 1:** Review the coping skills listed, making sure to explain any that are unfamiliar to students. As time allows, have the students demonstrate a couple of the coping skills. If students indicate they have used any of the skills before, allow them to share how the skill helped them feel.

    - **Activity 2:** Review the coping skills listed, making sure to explain any that are unfamiliar to students. In a fun twist on charades, have one student choose a coping skill from the sheet and act it out without speaking while the rest of the class guesses which strategy is being demonstrated. Rotate and let different students take turns acting out coping strategies.

    - **Bonus Activity:** Once students understand appropriate coping skills, using the **Alphabet Coping Skills Worksheet (Make Your Own)**, have them identify a coping skill they would use that starts with each letter of the alphabet. Encourage them to be creative. A variation of this activity is to instruct them to identify five coping skills that start with the same letter as their name.

    - **Bonus Activity:** Divide students into five groups. Hand out the **My Anxiety Coping Skills Worksheet** and instruct each group to brainstorm coping skills appropriate to use in their assigned setting: School, Home, Work, Friends/Social Settings, By Themselves. When the groups are finished, invite them to share their examples with the class. Point out the coping skills that can be used in multiple settings as particularly good strategies, since they have multiple applications.

56

15-MINUTE FOCUS
Anxiety Workbook: Tips and Strategies to Manage Anxiety, Build Resilience, and Foster Emotional Well-Being

Wrap Up & Assessment

5 MINUTES

- Ask students to circle 2–3 coping skills on the worksheet they will use when feeling anxious.

- Summarize the key points learned during the lessons about anxiety.

- Encourage students to remember that it is okay to feel anxious sometimes and that there are effective ways to cope with those feelings. If they need to talk more about their experiences with anxiety, remind them of the school staff there to support them (teacher, school counselor, school social worker, etc.) as well as their caregiver.

Note: Throughout the curriculum, be mindful of students who might be experiencing anxiety themselves. Create a supportive and safe environment for sharing and learning. If any student is consistently exhibiting signs of severe anxiety or distress, it is essential to involve school counselors or other appropriate personnel to provide additional support.

15-MINUTE FOCUS
Anxiety Workbook: Tips and Strategies to Manage Anxiety, Build Resilience, and Foster Emotional Well-Being

57

My Anxiety Coping Skills

Make a list of coping skills that are appropriate to use in each setting.

SCHOOL

_____   _____
_____   _____
_____   _____

HOME

_____   _____
_____   _____
_____   _____

WORK

_____   _____
_____   _____
_____   _____

WITH FRIENDS/SOCIAL SETTINGS

_____   _____
_____   _____
_____   _____

ALONE

_____   _____
_____   _____
_____   _____

General Interventions

Mindfulness Activities

Mindfulness is being aware of what is going on within and around you at a moment in time. It includes noticing how your body feels using your five senses and paying attention to one thing instead of trying to think about many things at one time. When we are being mindful, we are not making judgments or criticizing, we are simply being present. Mindfulness is a proven strategy to help increase focus, emotional regulation, and compassion while it also reduces anxiety and stress.[15]

The following mindfulness activities can be practiced with the class, in small groups, or with individual students.

Mindful Observation

Have the students pair up and give each pair a small object, such as a feather, a shell, or a smooth stone. Instruct them to observe the object carefully using their senses: "How does it feel? What colors do you see? Does it have a smell?" Students can share their observations without judgments.

Mindful Music

Inform students that they are going to pay attention to music in a different way today. As students sit comfortably in their chairs, instruct them listen to a song as it is played for one minute. No need to talk, write, or move around—just listen. Once the song has stopped, students will write down what they noticed, including what title they would give the song based on what they heard. Encourage them to write any thoughts they had while listening to the music, any feelings they noticed while listening, and any physical sensations or movements they felt during the song.

Body Scan

Guide students through a body scan, where they focus on each part of their body, starting from the toes and moving up to the head, noticing any tension and releasing it.

Guided Imagery

Lead students through guided imagery exercises, asking them to visualize peaceful scenes like a beach, forest, or mountain.

Mindful Walking

Take students outside for a mindful walking exercise, encouraging them to focus on the sensations of walking, such as the feel of the ground beneath their feet. Encourage them to notice what they see, hear, smell, and taste on their walk.

15-MINUTE FOCUS
Anxiety Workbook: Tips and Strategies to Manage Anxiety, Build Resilience, and Foster Emotional Well-Being

59

Mindful Movement

Introduce simple yoga or stretching exercises, guiding students to be present in the movement and sensations. Ask them to visualize their muscles stretching and bones spreading during the exercises. As they breathe in and out, remind them that their blood is carrying oxygen to their muscles allowing them to stretch longer.

Mindful Breathing

Teach students to focus on their breath, taking slow and deep breaths. They can place their hands on their belly to feel the rise and fall of each breath.

Mindful Listening

Have students close their eyes and listen carefully to different sounds, such as a bell ringing, birds chirping, or ambient noises.

Mindful Drawing and Coloring

Give students the opportunity to draw or doodle mindfully, encouraging them to focus on each stroke or detail. Provide coloring sheets and colored pencils, allowing students to engage in mindful coloring, concentrating on the colors and patterns.

Mindful Gratitude Practice

Have students write down or share something they are grateful for each day, fostering a positive mindset. Include how the act of being grateful impacts their overall attitude and outlook.

Mindful Journaling

Encourage students to keep a mindfulness journal, where they can write about their experiences, feelings, and insights related to mindfulness activities.

Mindful Compassion

Teach students a loving-kindness mantra or meditation where they send positive wishes and compassion to themselves and others.

Mindfulness Videos

There are many online resources for mindfulness videos. Some examples include:

- **GoNoodle**
  - Channel Flow
  - From Mindless to Mindful
    https://www.gonoodle.com/videos/lYVOAX/from-mindless-to-mindful
  - Swirling
    https://www.gonoodle.com/videos/eYxKjw/swirling

- Melting
  https://www.gonoodle.com/videos/r2rMeX/melting
- Let's Unwind
  https://www.gonoodle.com/videos/DXDN8w/lets-unwind

- **The Mindfulness Teacher**

  - Belly Breathing
    https://www.youtube.com/watch?v=RiMb2Bw4Ae8
  - Rainbow Relaxation
    https://www.youtube.com/watch?v=IIbBI-BT9c4

- **ClassDojo**

  - Mindful Breathing with Mojo
    https://ideas.classdojo.com/f/mindfulness-breathing/0
  - Mindful Movements
    https://ideas.classdojo.com/f/mindfulness-movements/0

15-MINUTE FOCUS
Anxiety Workbook: Tips and Strategies to Manage Anxiety, Build Resilience, and Foster Emotional Well-Being

61

Mindfulness Techniques

Mindful Observation

Mindful Music

Body Scan

Guided Imagery

Mindful Walking

Mindful Movement

Mindful Breathing

Mindful Listening

Mindful Drawing and Coloring

Mindful Gratitude Practice

Mindful Journaling

Mindful Compassion

Breathing Techniques to Reduce Anxiety

Breathing techniques are an effective and accessible way to reduce anxiety and promote relaxation. Here are some popular breathing exercises to help you calm your mind and body.

Belly Breathing

- Sit or lie down in a comfortable position.
- Place one hand on your chest and the other on your abdomen.
- Inhale deeply through your nose, allowing your abdomen to rise while keeping your chest relatively still.
- Exhale slowly and completely through your mouth or nose, feeling your abdomen fall.
- Repeat this process for several minutes, focusing on the rhythm of your breath.

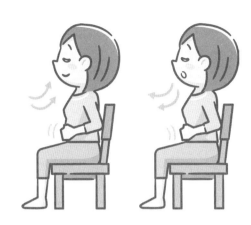

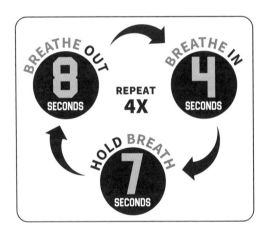

4-7-8 Breathing

- Close your mouth and inhale quietly through your nose to a count of four.
- Hold your breath for a count of seven.
- Exhale completely through your mouth to a count of eight.
- This is one breath cycle. Repeat for at least four cycles.

Square Breathing

- As you inhale slowly through your nose to a count of four, draw a horizontal line in front of you.
- Hold your breath for a count of four.
- Exhale slowly through your mouth to a count of four and draw a vertical line down from the end of the horizontal line.
- Pause and hold your breath for another count of four. Inhale slowly through your nose to a count of four and draw another horizontal line in the other direction.
- Hold your breath for a count of four.
- Exhale slowly through your mouth to a count of four and draw a vertical line up from the end of the bottom horizontal line to the top horizontal to complete the square.
- Repeat the cycle for several rounds.

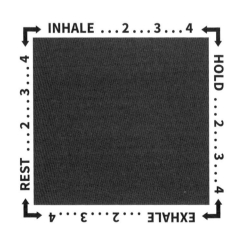

15-MINUTE FOCUS
Anxiety Workbook: Tips and Strategies to Manage Anxiety, Build Resilience, and Foster Emotional Well-Being

63

Bubble Breathing

- Inhale deeply through your nose.
- Purse your lips as if you were going to blow a bubble.
- Exhale slowly and gently through your pursed lips.
- The exhale should take twice as long as the inhale.
- Repeat for several breaths.

  If you have bubbles and can practice this outside, include some mindful observation watching the bubbles float away.

Visualization Breathing

- Close your eyes and imagine a peaceful and calming scene.
- As you inhale, visualize yourself absorbing the positive and calming elements of that scene.
- As you exhale, imagine releasing any tension, stress, or anxiety.
- Continue the visualization with each breath.

64

15-MINUTE FOCUS
Anxiety Workbook: Tips and Strategies to Manage Anxiety, Build Resilience, and Foster Emotional Well-Being

Breathing Techniques

Belly Breathing

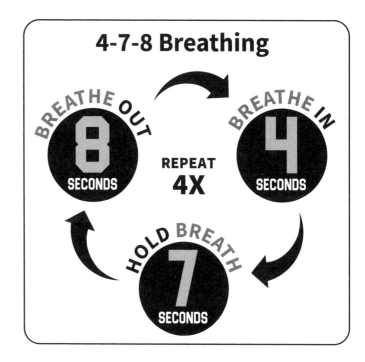

4-7-8 Breathing

BREATHE OUT **8** SECONDS

BREATHE IN **4** SECONDS

HOLD BREATH **7** SECONDS

REPEAT **4X**

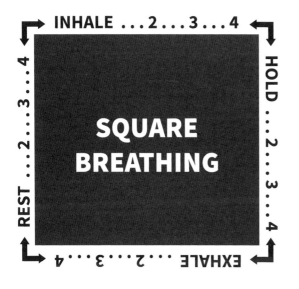

INHALE . . . 2 . . . 3 . . . 4

HOLD . . . 2 . . . 3 . . . 4

REST . . . 2 . . . 3 . . . 4

EXHALE . . . 2 . . . 3 . . . 4

SQUARE BREATHING

Bubble Breathing

Inhale deeply through your nose.

Purse your lips as if you were going to blow a bubble.

Exhale slowly and gently through your pursed lips.

Repeat for several breaths.

Visualization Breathing

- Close your eyes and imagine a peaceful and calming scene.
- As you inhale, visualize yourself absorbing the positive and calming elements of that scene.
- As you exhale, imagine releasing any tension, stress, or anxiety.
- Continue the visualization with each breath.

15-MINUTE FOCUS
Anxiety Workbook: Tips and Strategies to Manage Anxiety, Build Resilience, and Foster Emotional Well-Being

65

This is just a feeling.

It will pass.

I will accept the things I cannot control.

I am trying my best, and that is enough.

I am more than my anxiety.

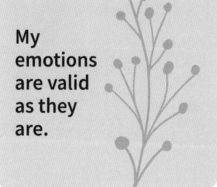

My emotions are valid as they are.

Not all thoughts are facts.

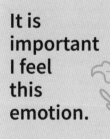

It is important I feel this emotion.

I have survived this before.

I can do it again.

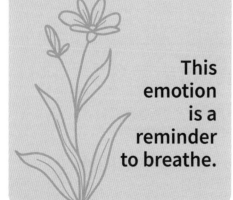

This emotion is a reminder to breathe.

Anxiety
COPING STATEMENTS

66

15-MINUTE FOCUS
Anxiety Workbook: Tips and Strategies to Manage Anxiety, Build Resilience, and Foster Emotional Well-Being

Caregiver Information on General Anxiety

Understanding and Supporting Your Child's Anxiety

As caregivers, we want the best for our children, and their emotional well-being is a top priority. Anxiety is a common challenge that many kids face at different stages of their lives, from elementary school to high school. It is essential to recognize the signs of anxiety and learn how to support our children through it.

What is Anxiety?

Anxiety is a response to stressful or unfamiliar situations. Anxiety is a feeling of worry or fear that everyone experiences from time to time. Anxiety is based in fear. It could be a fear of letting someone else down, a fear of letting ourselves down, or a fear associated with a threat to our physical, emotional, or social safety. Anxiety is a common part of life, and it is important to teach children appropriate coping skills they will use to successfully manage those uncomfortable feelings.

Some level of anxiety can be helpful in certain situations. However, when anxiety becomes an excessive concern about a potential triggering event or perceived threat to one's safety—one that interrupts our students' ability to engage in regular activities such as attending school, participating in extracurricular activities, or taking care of their physical needs—they may need additional support. Students may worry about threats they believe are real to their physical safety, emotional well-being, or social status, or relationships.

Symptoms of Anxiety

Anxiety can manifest differently in children of different ages. Here are some common symptoms to look out for:

Elementary School Students

- Restlessness and difficulty concentrating.
- Frequent complaints of stomachaches or headaches.
- Avoidance of certain situations, like going to school or social events.
- Trouble falling asleep or experiencing frequent nightmares.

Middle School Students

- Increased self-consciousness and concern about peer acceptance.
- Excessive worry about school performance and grades.
- Withdrawal from friends and social activities.
- Overthinking or catastrophic thinking (expecting the worst in every situation).

High School Students

- Intense fear of failure and uncertainty about the future.
- Panic attacks or physical symptoms like sweating, trembling, or rapid heartbeat.
- Social anxiety and fear of public speaking.
- Changes in eating or sleeping habits.

15-MINUTE FOCUS
Anxiety Workbook: Tips and Strategies to Manage Anxiety, Build Resilience, and Foster Emotional Well-Being

67

Strategies to Support Your Child

- **Create a safe environment:** Foster an open and non-judgmental space where your child feels comfortable expressing their feelings. Let them know it is okay to talk about anxiety and that you are there to listen and support them without judgment.

- **Validate their feelings:** Some children experience anxiety due to triggers that, as adults, we know are not probable or realistic. It is important to acknowledge that your child believes that they are real. Discounting the anxiety because the trigger is not likely will not reduce the anxiety in the moment. Wait until your child is calm and able to process through the likelihood of an event occurring.

- **Teach relaxation techniques:** Encourage your child to practice relaxation exercises like deep breathing, mindfulness, or Progressive Muscle Relaxation when they feel anxious. These techniques can help them manage stress.

- **Set realistic expectations:** Acknowledge your child's efforts rather than focusing solely on outcomes. Celebrate their progress and hard work, regardless of the end result.

- **Gradual exposure:** If your child is avoiding certain situations due to anxiety, work with them to take small steps toward facing their fears. Gradual exposure can help them build confidence and resilience.

- **Seek professional help if necessary:** If anxiety is significantly impacting your child's daily life and well-being, consider seeking support from a mental health professional experienced in working with children and adolescents.

Discussion Starters for Conversations with Your Child About Anxiety

Many children are afraid to talk about their feelings of anxiety. Having a trusted adult initiate the conversation can reduce their anxiety. The most effective discussions take place when the child is feeling calm and secure in a comfortable environment. Here are some questions that can help you start conversations with your child about anxiety they may be experiencing:

- "I noticed you seem a bit worried lately. Would you like to talk about it?"
- "It's okay to feel anxious sometimes. Is there anything specific that's bothering you?"
- "How do you think we can handle anxiety when it starts to feel overwhelming?"
- "What are some things that make you feel calm and happy when you're feeling anxious?"
- "Remember, I'm always here for you. Is there anything I can do to help you feel better?"

Strategies for Caregivers to Reduce Anxiety and Stress

As caregivers, your child will often look to you to see how you handle anxiety. Practicing appropriate coping skills for yourself provides your child with a healthy example. Watching you practice good coping strategies also helps them understand that they are not alone in their experience with anxiety. Here are some strategies that you can use for yourself and with your child to manage anxiety:

- **Practice self-care:** Make time for activities that bring you joy and relaxation. Whether it's reading, exercise, or spending time with loved ones, taking care of yourself sets a positive example for your child.

- **Limit media exposure:** Constant exposure to negative news and social media can contribute to anxiety. Set boundaries and create technology-free zones to promote a healthy balance.

68

15-MINUTE FOCUS
Anxiety Workbook: Tips and Strategies to Manage Anxiety, Build Resilience, and Foster Emotional Well-Being

- **Seek support:** Talk to friends, family, or a mental health professional if you need someone to confide in or seek advice from.
- **Model healthy coping strategies:** Demonstrate healthy ways to cope with stress, such as taking breaks, problem-solving, or using positive affirmations.

By understanding anxiety and employing effective strategies, caregivers can provide crucial support to their children during challenging times. Open communication, empathy, and encouragement will foster a strong sense of resilience and well-being in your child as they navigate their way through elementary, middle, and high school. Remember that taking care of your own well-being is equally important, as it enables you to be a source of strength and guidance for your child.

Each child's experience is unique, and they may need varying levels of support. By understanding their anxieties and being proactive in supporting them, we can help our children navigate these experiences with greater confidence and resilience. If you or your child needs additional assistance, please reach out to the school counselor for support. We are here to partner with you for your students' success.

15-MINUTE FOCUS
Anxiety Workbook: Tips and Strategies to Manage Anxiety, Build Resilience, and Foster Emotional Well-Being

69

Counseling Interventions for General Anxiety

Many students who experience anxiety will respond positively to the universal education and interventions provided through school-wide approaches, classroom lessons and activities, and classroom accommodations and considerations. Other students with more moderate symptoms, frequent and ongoing episodes, or with greater disruption to their daily functioning, will need additional, targeted support in order to learn and practice skills and strategies to manage and reduce their anxiety. Trained school personnel such as school counselors, school social workers, or school psychologists can provide professional interventions like small group counseling, individual counseling, caregiver consultation, and referral for community resources. These educators may collaborate with school-based community mental health partners to deliver evidence-based supports to students enduring issues with anxiety.

In this chapter we will explore Cognitive Behavioral Therapy (CBT) and individual counseling interventions to support students experiencing anxiety.

Cognitive Behavioral Therapy

CBT has been proven to be an effective theoretical framework for reducing anxiety.[16] The tenets of CBT suggest that our thoughts are influenced by our feelings which then drive how we behave. If we want to change our behavior, CBT proposes that we must change dysfunctional thinking to access new emotions. For example, when a student earns a poor grade on an assignment (the trigger), they believe they are never going to pass the course (dysfunctional belief). They feel worried and hopeless (feelings) and quit taking notes in class (problematic behavior). Using CBT, the school counselor can help the student restructure their dysfunctional beliefs by helping them identify several actions that they can take to mitigate the poor grade and still pass the course. When the student recognizes that they have options, they notice that they no longer feel worried and hopeless. They feel relieved and hopeful and are motivated to pay attention in class.

With CBT, anxious students can remember that there are strategies they can use to control what is happening in their bodies. Instead of being worried, they begin to feel empowered. That positive feeling leads to more effective behavior management. CBT does not get rid of anxiety, but it does help to redefine the relationship students have with their symptoms. By reducing the fears associated with anxiety, students can lessen the power it exerts over them. CBT has been proven to be a helpful approach in both individual and group counseling.

The following lessons are designed to teach students about CBT and how it can help them manage and reduce anxiety.

70

15-MINUTE FOCUS
Anxiety Workbook: Tips and Strategies to Manage Anxiety, Build Resilience, and Foster Emotional Well-Being

"Think-Feel-Do" Cycle: Understanding CBT

ELEMENTARY, MIDDLE, HIGH

MATERIALS	• "Think-Feel-Do" Cycle: Understanding CBT Handout (Elementary or Middle/High)

"Think-Feel-Do" Cycle

The **"Think-Feel-Do" Cycle: Understanding CBT Handout** for Elementary and Middle/High can help students understand the relationships between thoughts, feelings, and behaviors. Have students work through non-threatening or non-anxiety-inducing situations first.

- Ask the students to name their favorite food, person, pet, etc. When they see that favorite thing, ask them how they feel. Encourage them to point to the "Feelings" section of the worksheet while they are sharing.

- Next ask them to identify what thoughts they have when they see their favorite thing. As they describe their thoughts, they should point to the "Thoughts" section.

- Finally, ask them what they do when they see that favorite thing. For example, if they see their favorite person, do they wave, walk toward them, run, and give them a hug, etc.? The student should point to the "Behaviors" section as they describe their actions.

- Once they have identified each section, ask them to start the "Thoughts" section.

   What if you think about your favorite thing? How do you feel? Do you feel happy, excited, etc.? What is your action? Do you send them a message? Go and see them? If you think about your favorite food, do you go to the kitchen to get some?

   This cycle happens almost automatically. When you see your favorite pet, you do not stop and ask yourself "How do I feel when I see my puppy?" You often feel joy and rush to greet your dog or welcome the dog as it greets you.

- When students understand the cycle, repeat the process with a situation that triggers anxiety. Help students recognize how thoughts, feelings, and behaviors are interdependent on one another.

- Challenge them to change a feeling, thought, or behavior in the cycle and imagine how it might change the other two.

15-MINUTE FOCUS
Anxiety Workbook: Tips and Strategies to Manage Anxiety, Build Resilience, and Foster Emotional Well-Being

71

"Think-Feel-Do" Cycle: Understanding CBT (Elementary)

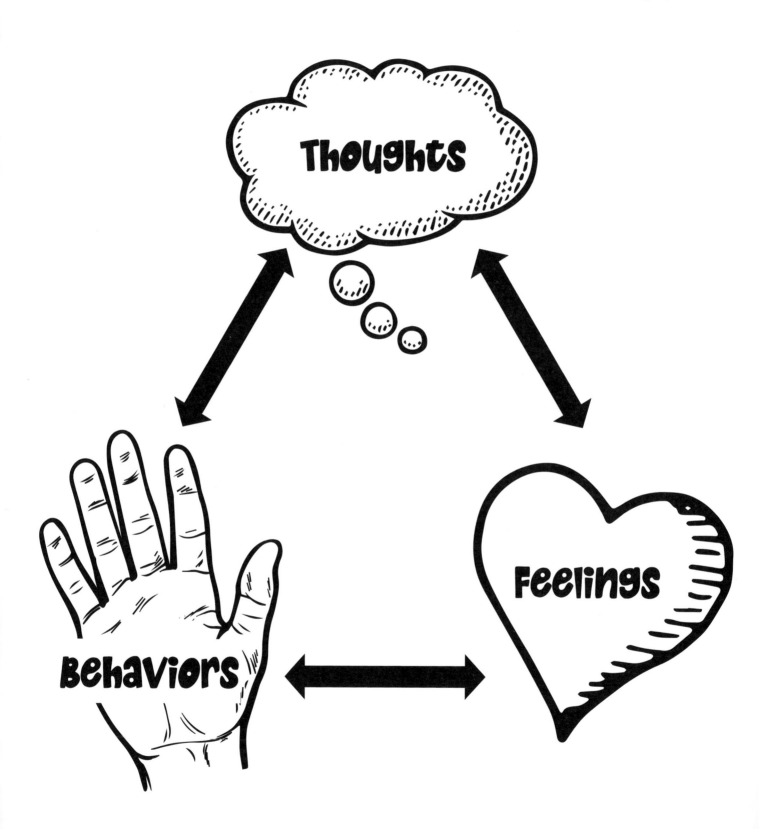

"Think-Feel-Do" Cycle:
Understanding CBT (Middle/High)

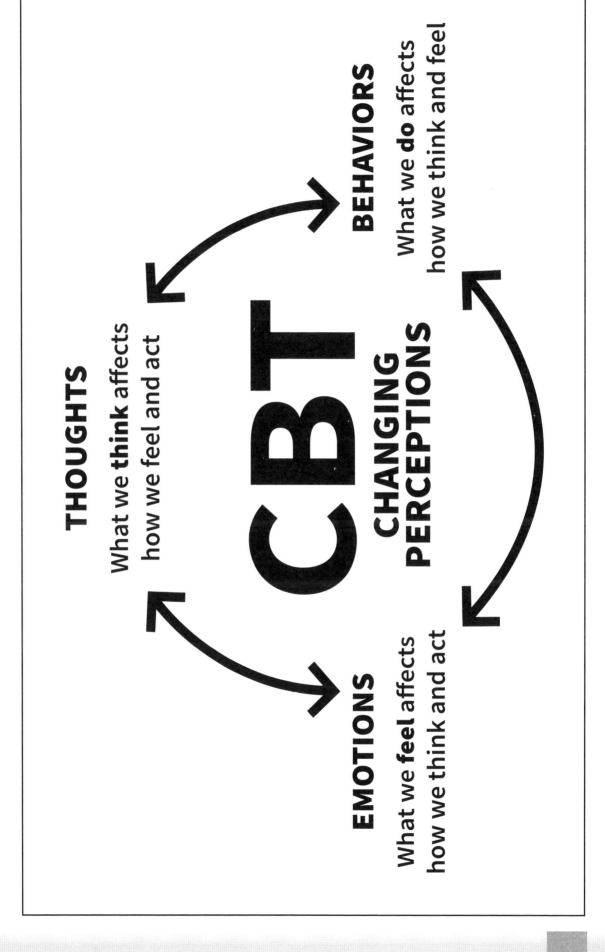

THOUGHTS
What we **think** affects how we feel and act

CBT

CHANGING PERCEPTIONS

BEHAVIORS
What we **do** affects how we think and feel

EMOTIONS
What we **feel** affects how we think and act

15-MINUTE FOCUS
Anxiety Workbook: Tips and Strategies to Manage Anxiety, Build Resilience, and Foster Emotional Well-Being

73

Exchanging Thoughts

MIDDLE, HIGH

MATERIALS	• Exchanging Thoughts Worksheet

Exchange Negative Thoughts for Positive Ones

This activity helps students practice replacing learned negative thoughts with new positive ones.

When we continue to allow negative thoughts to control our feelings and behaviors over time, they create automatic pathways in our brain. We respond automatically to those negative thoughts, which typically leads to increased anxiety and discomfort.

CBT can help us to recreate pathways by replacing those negative thoughts with positive ones. Much like creating a new habit, it takes work to stop the negative thinking, but with practice and support, students (and adults) can shift our thoughts and subsequently our feelings to more positive, self-accepting ones that will reduce anxiety.

- In this activity, help students identify anxious thoughts they have. For example, common anxious thoughts for high school students often are related to meeting expectations. The following thoughts may serve to spark their memory of specific anxious thoughts:

  "I'll never pass my math test."

  "I'm not good enough to make the basketball team."

  "Nobody likes me here. I will never have any friends."

  "My family can't afford to buy me the (coolest trend). People will judge me and think I am not good enough."

  "I am so afraid of speaking in front of people. I can't do the presentation for history class. My teacher will never understand."

- Typically, these negative thoughts are exaggerated or overgeneralized. Students will use words like always, never, can't, won't, etc. These are **cognitive distortions** that reinforce negative beliefs that are likely not true. Challenging the veracity of these statements will help students recognize that their feelings and subsequent behaviors are based on untrue thoughts.

- Challenging the student's negative thought, "I am so afraid of speaking in front of people. I can't do the presentation for history class. My teacher will never understand." could look like this:

74

15-MINUTE FOCUS
Anxiety Workbook: Tips and Strategies to Manage Anxiety, Build Resilience, and Foster Emotional Well-Being

Counselor: *What I hear you say is that speaking in front of the class would be difficult for you and you do not think that the teacher can understand your situation. What reasons do you have for thinking that the teacher will never understand your situation?*

Student: *Well, the assignment is that we have to do an oral presentation, so I'm sure that she will make me do it. I should just go ahead and tell her to give me a zero.*

Counselor: *Have you seen the teacher show understanding to you or another student for any other reason?*

Student: *She did let Stephen leave class early when he was on crutches after he hurt his knee.*

Counselor: *So, your teacher has shown that she is capable of understanding situations when students can't follow the regular rules or procedures?*

Student: *I guess so.*

Counselor: *I'm wondering if it is possible that your teacher might show you some understanding if you made her aware of your anxiety about speaking in front of the class. Would that be a true statement?*

Student: *Yeah, I guess it's possible. Yes, it is true.*

Counselor: *Instead of saying that your teacher will never understand, how might you change your negative statement to be more accurate and more positive?*

Student: *What if I said, "I am so afraid of speaking in front of people. I can't do the presentation for history class. Maybe if I talk to my teacher about my anxiety, she will understand and work with me?"*

Counselor: *Is that a true statement?*

Student: *Yes*

Counselor: *That is a great exchange. I wonder if it also gives you a little less anxiety about the situation because now you have an action that you can take that could lead to a positive resolution.*

- Using the **Exchanging Thoughts Worksheet**, have the student practice exchanging positive thoughts for negative ones. Remind them that it will take some time for their brain to not automatically go to the negative thoughts, but with practice they can make that switch and reduce their anxiety.

15-MINUTE FOCUS
Anxiety Workbook: Tips and Strategies to Manage Anxiety, Build Resilience, and Foster Emotional Well-Being

75

Exchanging Thoughts

Write down three anxious thoughts that you have often. Think of a positive thought with which to exchange each of them. The next time an anxious thought comes into your mind, remind yourself of the positive thought instead.

EXAMPLE:

Anxious Thought: I don't understand this math, and I am going to fail the test.

Positive Thought: I am having trouble understanding this math, but I can ask for help and then practice so that I am ready for the test.

SCHOOL

Anxious Thought: _____

_____

Positive Thought: _____

_____

HOME

Anxious Thought: _____

_____

Positive Thought: _____

_____

FRIENDS

Anxious Thought: _____

_____

Positive Thought: _____

_____

_____

Positive Associations

MIDDLE, HIGH

MATERIALS | • Positive Associations Worksheet

Making Positive Associations

Anxiety is rooted in fear. When your amygdala senses a threat and feels afraid, it takes over and tries to protect you. For example, imagine someone has anxiety about fire. If all their brain knows about fire is that it scares them, when they see fire, their amygdala is going think "DANGER – FIRE!" If we recognize there are different meanings for fire, our thinking brain (the cerebrum) will have to stay in charge to decide whether it is dangerous or not.

Pass out the **Positive Associations Worksheet**. In this activity,

- Ask the student to identify a potential trigger of their anxiety.
- Next, they will recognize various meanings that the trigger will have. They should include the meaning that represents the threat the trigger represents, but also encourage them to think broadly of other possible meanings. You may assist them in researching the trigger to determine potential meanings.
- As the student identifies new representations for the trigger, help them to make positive associations with the new meanings. They can learn that their trigger does not always have to lead to feelings of anxiety.

15-MINUTE FOCUS
Anxiety Workbook: Tips and Strategies to Manage Anxiety, Build Resilience, and Foster Emotional Well-Being

77

Positive Association

Identify something that triggers feelings of anxiety, and write it in the center circle. In one of the outer circles, write what the trigger represents that scares you. For example, if your trigger is fire, write 'Fire' in the center circle. If you are afraid of getting burned, then in one of the outer circles, write 'Getting Burned.' In the remaining circles, brainstorm other meanings of the trigger. Fire could represent warmth, a cooking source, creating a soft mood, campfire, etc.

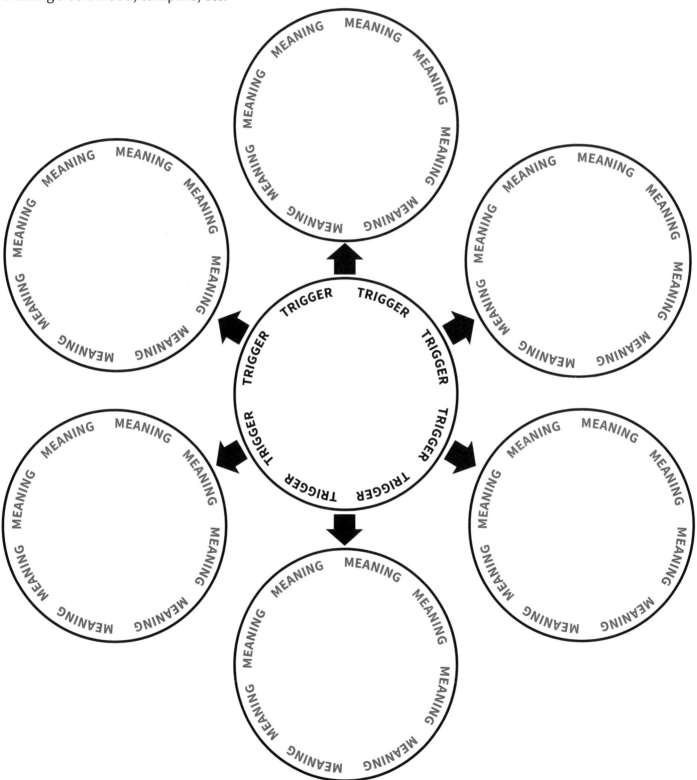

Individual Counseling Interventions for Students Experiencing General Anxiety

The following worksheets can be used with individual students to help them learn about anxiety, understand their own experience with anxiety, identify strategies to better manage their anxiety, and practice coping skills to reduce their anxiety. Instructions and probing questions to help students process the content of activity follow below.

How Anxiety Feels In My Body

(Elementary, Middle, High)

Give the student the **How Anxiety Feels in My Body Worksheet**. They will identify where they feel anxiety in their body. The student should write anxiety symptoms they experience in the bubbles, then draw lines from each bubble to where they feel each symptom in their body. For emotional symptoms such as sadness, they could draw a line to their heart. For behavioral symptoms such as running away, they can draw a line to their feet. It is okay for the student to draw more than one line to the same area of the body.

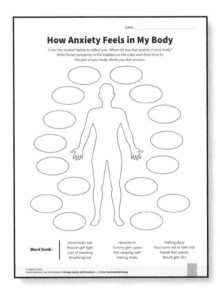

Once the student has identified where they feel their symptoms, process the activity with them with questions such as:

- How is knowing what anxiety feels like in your body important?
- How does knowing your symptoms help you manage your anxiety?
- How does knowing your symptoms help you identify your anxiety triggers?

Managing My Anxiety

(Elementary)

There are two versions of this activity designed to be developmentally appropriate for each student group.

The elementary version allows the student to develop awareness of how they feel when they express different levels of anxiety. Give the student the **Managing My Anxiety Worksheet (Elementary)**. Brainstorm what coping skills they can use to move from high to mild anxiety and mild anxiety to no anxiety. Encourage them to practice those coping skills to manage their anxiety.

15-MINUTE FOCUS
Anxiety Workbook: Tips and Strategies to Manage Anxiety, Build Resilience, and Foster Emotional Well-Being

79

Managing My Anxiety

(Middle, High)

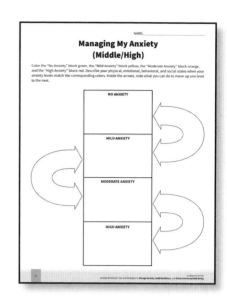

The middle and high school version of this activity will help the student understand that taking one step from high levels of anxiety to lower levels is a more effective way of managing their anxiety than trying to get rid of it all at once.

Hand out the **Managing My Anxiety Worksheet (Middle/High)**. The student will describe themselves when they have no anxiety, mild anxiety, moderate anxiety, and high anxiety. On the arrows, help them identify actions they can take to move to the next level. Discuss the importance of taking one step at a time. It can be overwhelming to try to get from red to green. Moving from red to orange is much more manageable. Consider talking through what it looks like when your anxiety begins to escalate, going from green to yellow, yellow to orange, and orange to red. Recognizing the smaller steps can help you to implement strategies to prevent you from getting all the way to red.

My Personal Safety Plan

(Elementary, Middle, High)

There are two versions of this activity designed to be developmentally appropriate for each student group.

Give the student the age-appropriate **My Personal Safety Plan Worksheet**. This activity helps the student prepare for their anxiety by recognizing the symptoms they experience as warning signs that the anxiety is coming, identifying specific coping skills they can use to manage and reduce their anxiety, and name the resources that are available to them if they need help. Stress that having a plan in place before they start to feel the anxiety is a good strategy to decrease the effect of the fear the trigger causes.

Information is the Antidote to Fear

(Older Elementary, Middle, High)

Anxiety is rooted in fear. Fear thrives in "not knowing." When we discover information about the thing that we are afraid of, the fear is not so scary.

Using the **Information is the Antidote to Fear Worksheet**, the student will name a fear that is driving their anxiety. Help the student identify what factors are contributing to the situation such as personal, social, or environmental issues. What does the student not know about the fear? What is contributing to their worry or stress? Help them identify where they can access that information.

Next, assist the student in recognizing what factors of the situation are within their control. Trying to control things that they cannot actually increases their anxiety.

Finally, work with the student to develop a plan of action to seek the information needed to diminish the power of their fear and reduce their anxiety.

Looking at Anxiety Through a Different Lens

(Older Elementary, Middle, High)

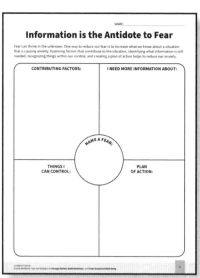

What triggers anxiety in one person may not trigger anxiety for another. One strategy for helping students manage and reduce their anxiety is to help them view their triggers differently. Rather than seeing the trigger as a threat, if they can reframe it as something either innocuous or even positive, then the trigger loses its potential to set off the amygdala and start the Fight, Flight, Freeze, Fawn response.

Give the student the **Looking at Anxiety Through a Different Lens Worksheet**. Help the student see both the duck and bunny in the picture if they are unable on their own. Use the picture to explain that their trigger might only look harmful at first, but there may be another way to look at it. The student will then identify a trigger. Instruct them to identify the reason this activity makes them anxious.

Next, assist them in exploring how this activity could be harmless or even exciting. Encourage the student to imagine how it would feel to view the trigger as exciting instead of a threat. Do they still feel as anxious?

15-MINUTE FOCUS
Anxiety Workbook: Tips and Strategies to Manage Anxiety, Build Resilience, and Foster Emotional Well-Being

81

Anxiety Triggers

(Elementary)

There are two versions of this activity designed to be developmentally appropriate for each student group.

The **Anxiety Triggers Worksheet (Elementary)** helps elementary students identify what is triggering their anxiety and choose coping skills to better manage and reduce their anxious feelings. Utilizing red and green colors, the student will identify one trigger in each of the flags. They can use examples from the box or one of their own. They will color those flags red to indicate that they want to stop the feelings the triggers cause.

Using the **Coping Skills Picture List Handout,** show the student that using a smart coping skill can help stop those anxious feelings so that they can get going again. Encourage the student to choose a coping skill for each trigger they identified. They will write the coping skill in the second set of flags and color those green.

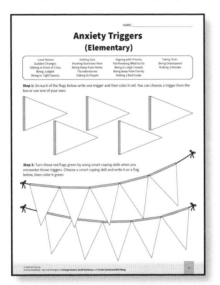

(Middle, High)

The **Anxiety Triggers Worksheet (Middle/High)** will help middle and high school students identify the activities and events that trigger different levels of anxiety. Once the student identifies the triggers with the highest scores, work with them to uncover what is happening with those triggers to cause their distress. Then develop smart coping strategies the student can use when those events occur. Refer to the **50 Coping Skills Handout** for ideas.

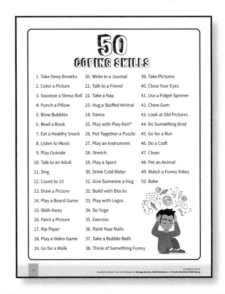

82

15-MINUTE FOCUS
Anxiety Workbook: Tips and Strategies to Manage Anxiety, Build Resilience, and Foster Emotional Well-Being

Learning From the Past

(Older Elementary, Middle, High)

In this activity, the student will explore previous experiences with anxiety. Using the **Learning From the Past Worksheet**, have the student describe a time when they were anxious or worried. Assist them in recognizing strategies and actions that helped them manage and get through the situation. The student should also identify things that were not helpful in reducing their anxiety. Remind the student that they can use successful strategies and coping skills when they feel anxiety again. When the student uses those strategies, they can also be a cue that the student has endured an uncomfortable moment before and use that knowledge to persevere again.

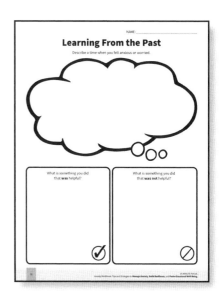

You Are Not Your Anxiety

(Older Elementary, Middle)

Ask the student to close their eyes and think about their anxiety or worry for one minute, paying attention to what they feel. Help them use their five senses to describe their anxiety.

Pass out the **You Are Not Your Anxiety Worksheet**. Separating themselves from their anxiety can show students that they are not their worry/anxiety. It can reduce feelings that they are bad or unworthy. When they see their anxiety outside of themselves, they can focus on addressing it more easily than if they think they are themselves the problem.

Once they have externalized their anxiety, begin assisting them in identifying potential cognitive distortions that are contributing to negative feelings and behaviors.

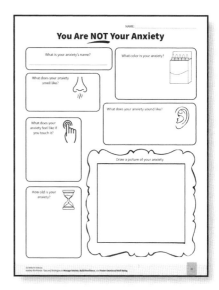

Write a Story

(Middle, High)

The student will learn strategies to manage their anxiety by writing a story using their anxiety as a character. Separating themselves from their anxiety can show the student that they are not their worry/anxiety. It can reduce feelings that they are bad or unworthy. When they see their anxiety outside of themselves, they can focus on addressing it more easily than if they think they are themselves the problem.

Use the following prompts to help the student create a story about their anxiety.

- *Describe your anxiety as a character in a story or movie. Include characteristics such as:*
  - *Size*
  - *Color*
  - *Body type*

15-MINUTE FOCUS
Anxiety Workbook: Tips and Strategies to Manage Anxiety, Build Resilience, and Foster Emotional Well-Being

83

- *Special features*
- *How it communicates*
- *How it moves*
- *Special skills, talents, or powers*

- *What is your anxiety's name?*
- *What is (anxiety name)'s purpose or goal?*
- *What kinds of situations give (anxiety's name) power or energy?*
- *Let's imagine a character that can defeat or control (anxiety's name). Describe that character using the same characteristics:*
  - *Size*
  - *Color*
  - *Body type*
  - *Special features*
  - *How it communicates*
  - *How it moves*
  - *Special skills, talents, powers*

(You may need to remind the student that this character needs to have knowledge/skills/powers to defeat the anxiety. This is a good time to reinforce appropriate prevention and coping. Once the student has described a character with skills to manage or control the anxiety, move on.)

- *What is this character's name?*
- *You now have two really interesting characters. Now let's imagine that as the story begins (anxiety's name) is looking for someone to bother. When, all of a sudden, (choose one of the situations that the student identified as giving anxiety power) happens.*
- *Who might get hurt?*
- *What happens next?*
- *How can (hero character) help? What does he/she do?*

Encourage the student to explore how using appropriate skills and knowledge can manage or control the anxiety.

Capture the details of the story. After the session the student can either write the full story and illustrate it on paper, electronically, as a presentation, etc. This will allow them to keep it as a reminder of how they can manage their own anxiety.

After the student finishes the story, process the experience with them:

- What did it feel like when (hero's name) defeated (anxiety's name)?
- How are you like (hero's name)?
- What things did (hero's name) do that you could also do when you feel anxious?

Managing My Anxiety
(Elementary)

Color the emoji the color that best matches how you feel at each level of anxiety. For "No Anxiety," color the emoji green. For "Mild Anxiety," color it yellow. For "High Anxiety," color it red.

 **NO ANXIETY**

CALM

HAPPY

LAUGHING

 **MILD ANXIETY**

NERVOUS

NAUSEOUS

WORRIED

 **HIGH ANXIETY**

OVERWHELMED

SCARED

CRYING

Draw or write coping skills you can do to move towards No Anxiety.

15-MINUTE FOCUS
Anxiety Workbook: Tips and Strategies to Manage Anxiety, Build Resilience, and Foster Emotional Well-Being

85

Managing My Anxiety
(Middle/High)

Color the "No Anxiety" block green, the "Mild Anxiety" block yellow, the "Moderate Anxiety" block orange, and the "High Anxiety" block red. Describe your physical, emotional, behavioral, and social states when your anxiety levels match the corresponding colors. Inside the arrows, note what you can do to move up one level to the next.

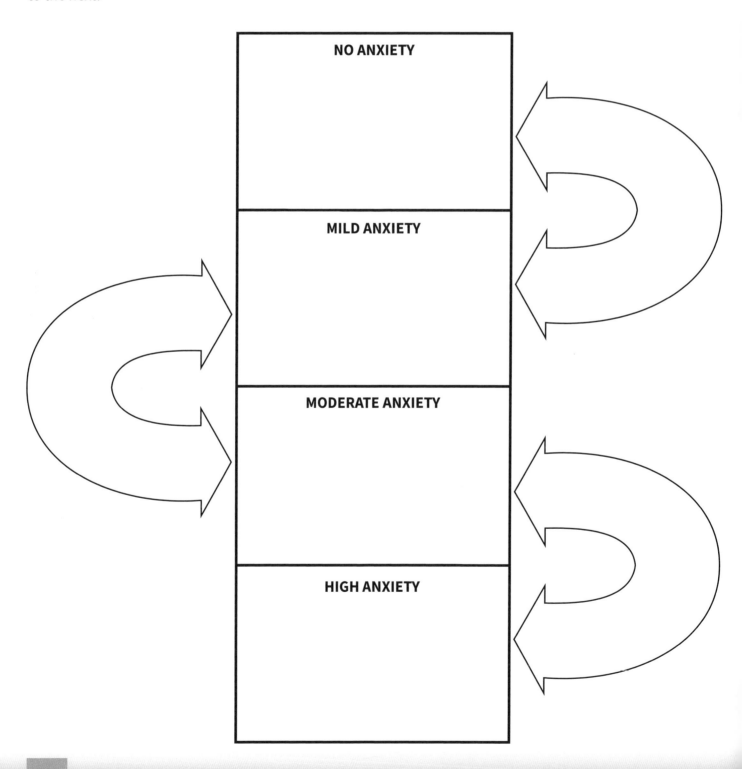

MY PERSONAL SAFETY PLAN

ELEMENTARY

WHEN I NOTICE MY BODY FEELS:

I CAN

TAKE CARE OF MYSELF BY:

GET HELP FROM:

15-MINUTE FOCUS
Anxiety Workbook: Tips and Strategies to Manage Anxiety, Build Resilience, and Foster Emotional Well-Being

87

MY PERSONAL SAFETY PLAN
MIDDLE/HIGH

I KNOW I'M TRIGGERED WHEN I NOTICE:

_____

_____

_____

_____

_____

_____

SOME GOOD WAYS TO DISTRACT MYSELF ARE:

THINGS THAT HELP ME WHEN I FEEL THIS WAY ARE:

WAYS I KEEP MYSELF SAFE:

_____

_____

_____

_____

_____

_____

SOME SAFE PEOPLE I CAN TALK TO ARE:

_____

_____

_____

_____

_____

OTHER RESOURCES I CAN USE TO GET MYSELF CARE:

1

2

3
CRISIS TEXT LINE: TEXT HOME TO 741741

Information is the Antidote to Fear

Fear can thrive in the unknown. One way to reduce our fear is to increase what we know about a situation that is causing anxiety. Exploring factors that contribute to the situation, identifying what information is still needed, recognizing things within our control, and creating a plan of action helps to reduce our anxiety.

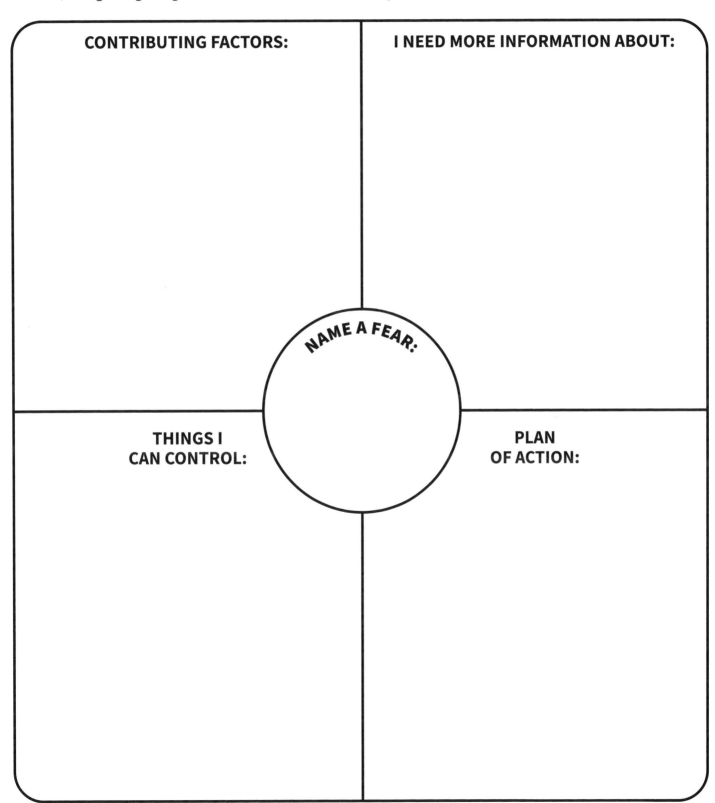

CONTRIBUTING FACTORS:

I NEED MORE INFORMATION ABOUT:

NAME A FEAR:

THINGS I CAN CONTROL:

PLAN OF ACTION:

15-MINUTE FOCUS
Anxiety Workbook: Tips and Strategies to Manage Anxiety, Build Resilience, and Foster Emotional Well-Being

89

Looking at Anxiety Through a Different Lens

What do you see when you look at the image here? A duck or a rabbit? Two people can look at the same image and see two different things. The same is true about the things that can cause us anxiety. What makes one person nervous can get another one excited, or even leave someone else unaffected.

Just as you are not wrong if you did not see both the bunny and the duck at first, you are not wrong for feeling anxious about something that others do not. When we look at something from another person's perspective, it gives us an opportunity to view the things that trigger our anxiety in a different way. That new perspective of the anxiety trigger can reduce its control over us.

ANXIETY CAUSING ACTIVITY:

THIS MAKES ME ANXIOUS BECAUSE:

THIS COULD BE EXCITING BECAUSE:

90

15-MINUTE FOCUS
Anxiety Workbook: Tips and Strategies to Manage Anxiety, Build Resilience, and Foster Emotional Well-Being

Anxiety Triggers
(Elementary)

Loud Noises	Getting Sick	Arguing with Friends	Taking Tests
Sudden Changes	Meeting Someone New	Not Knowing What to Do	Being Unprepared
Talking in Front of Class	Being Away from Home	Being in Large Crowds	Making a Mistake
Being Judged	Thunderstorms	Being Away from Family	
Being in Tight Spaces	Talking to People	Making a Bad Grade	

Step 1: On each of the flags below write one trigger and then color it red. You can choose a trigger from the box or use one of your own.

Step 2: Turn those red flags green by using smart coping skills when you encounter those triggers. Choose a smart coping skill and write it on a flag below, then color it green.

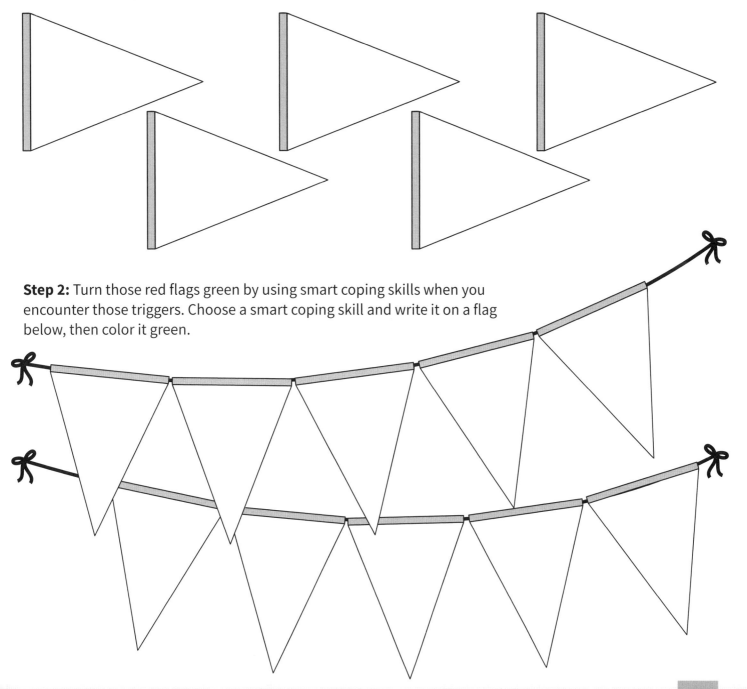

15-MINUTE FOCUS
Anxiety Workbook: Tips and Strategies to Manage Anxiety, Build Resilience, and Foster Emotional Well-Being

91

Anxiety Triggers
(Middle/High)

An anxiety trigger is something that happens to make you feel anxious.

Step 1: Review this list and write the number on this scale of 0 to 10 that matches how the activity makes you feel.

Step 2: For all triggers that scored 6 or higher write a coping skill you can use when you encounter that trigger.

ANXIETY LEVEL

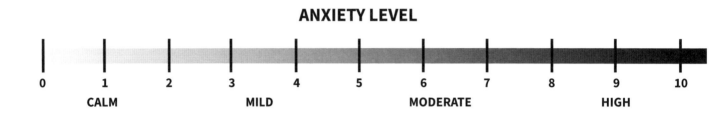

| 0 | 1 | 2 | 3 | 4 | 5 | 6 | 7 | 8 | 9 | 10 |
| CALM | | MILD | | | | MODERATE | | | HIGH | |

SCORE	TRIGGER	COPING SKILLS
	Being in a large crowd of people	
	Going to a place for the first time	
	Loud noises or raised voices	
	Being in tight spaces	
	Being in wide open spaces	
	Having too much to do	
	Giving a presentation in class	
	Working as a part of a group	
	Performing in front of others	
	Not feeling prepared	
	Getting a bad grade	
	Having to change up my routine	
	Thinking about college	
	Not knowing what career I want	
	Not having enough money	

92

15-MINUTE FOCUS
Anxiety Workbook: Tips and Strategies to Manage Anxiety, Build Resilience, and Foster Emotional Well-Being

	Disappointing someone	
	Not knowing what is going to happen	
	Family stress	
	Having to make decisions	
	My health	
	Responsibilities at home	
	Conflict in relationships	
	Having conversations with peers or adults	
	Being around certain people	
	Social media	
	Pressure to fit in	
	Meeting new people	
	Rumors being spread about me	
	Making new friends	
	Friends not talking to/texting me	
	Talking to someone I have a crush on	
	Feeling left out by friends	
	Being away from my phone	
	Watching the news	
	School violence	
	Bullying	
	My job, boss, or co-workers	
	Other people's expectations of me	
	A sick family member or friend	
	Changes in my body or weight	
	Interacting with a certain family member	
	Transportation	

15-MINUTE FOCUS
Anxiety Workbook: Tips and Strategies to Manage Anxiety, Build Resilience, and Foster Emotional Well-Being

93

Learning From the Past

Describe a time when you felt anxious or worried.

What is something you did that **was** helpful?	What is something you did that **was not** helpful?

NAME:_____

You Are NOT Your Anxiety

What is your anxiety's name?

_____

What color is your anxiety?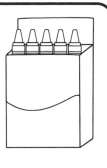

What does your anxiety smell like?

What does your anxiety sound like?

What does your anxiety feel like if you touch it?

Draw a picture of your anxiety.

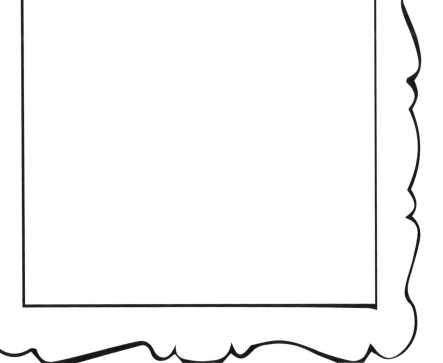

How old is your anxiety?

15-MINUTE FOCUS
Anxiety Workbook: Tips and Strategies to Manage Anxiety, Build Resilience, and Foster Emotional Well-Being

Individual Counseling Interventions for General Anxiety Related to School Safety

Anxiety related to school safety refers to the fear, worry, and distress experienced by students in response to concerns about their safety within the school environment. This anxiety can be triggered by a variety of factors, including school shootings, bullying, natural disasters, or other real or perceived safety threats. Students expressing anxiety due to issues related to safety at school do not have to experience threats to their safety directly. They can be impacted through vicarious trauma, exposure to distressing events through media, social media, or witnessing them happening in nearby communities. Elementary, middle, and high school students may develop anxiety about their safety at school with various emotional, physical, and behavioral symptoms.

Symptoms of Anxiety Related to Safety at School

Symptoms of anxiety related to safety at school can range in intensity from mild to severe, and may vary from one student to another:

Mild Symptoms

- Occasional worry or unease about their safety at school.
- Mild vigilance and increased awareness of surroundings.
- Mild avoidance of specific places or situations within the school building or campus.

Moderate Symptoms

- Increased and persistent anxiety about safety at school.
- Heightened sensitivity to safety-related news or discussions.
- Moderate avoidance of certain activities, locations, or school events.

Severe Symptoms

- Intense fear, dread, or panic about attending school due to safety concerns.
- Severe avoidance behaviors, such as refusing to attend school altogether.
- Frequent nightmares or intrusive thoughts related to threats to their safety at school.
- Physical symptoms such as rapid heartbeat, sweating, and gastrointestinal distress.

It is also common for students experiencing anxiety related to safety issues to exhibit symptoms of **separation anxiety**. They often seek security in loved ones and do not want to part with them to attend school or other activities. Safety drills, lockdowns, and the presence of law enforcement meant to protect students can serve as a reminder that their safety is at risk. If their anxiety originates from a weather-related incident or natural disaster, they will likely be hypersensitive during inclement weather.

Students whose threats to safety are rooted in issues of bullying and harassment may exhibit symptoms similar to **social anxiety**. Their fear of judgment from others drives them to make themselves unseen. These students will avoid engaging in interactions that raise the possibility of academic, physical, or social evaluation.

96

15-MINUTE FOCUS
Anxiety Workbook: Tips and Strategies to Manage Anxiety, Build Resilience, and Foster Emotional Well-Being

Because the nature of anxiety related to school safety is unique to each student, individual counseling interventions are recommended. Activities from the chapters on social anxiety and separation anxiety could be utilized if larger groups of students share similar experiences.

Individual counseling using Cognitive Behavioral Therapy with a trauma-focused approach has shown efficacy in working with students who have experienced traumatic events such as natural disasters, violence, and bullying.[17] **Trauma-Focused Cognitive Behavioral Therapy (TF-CBT)** utilizes CBT principles with sensitivity to specific factors associated with traumatic experiences. TF-CBT counseling includes:

- teaching the student about typical reactions to traumatic experiences to reduce feelings of guilt or responsibility for what happened.
- practicing coping skills such as deep breathing, mindfulness, and relaxation techniques.
- challenging faulty thinking or cognitive distortions and replacing those with kind, confidence-building thoughts based on facts and healthy expectations for oneself.
- learning strategies to regulate emotions more effectively.[18]

These interventions support the student in rebuilding their sense of trust and reaffirm their safety and security.

Creative Arts Techniques

(Elementary, Middle, High)

In addition to TF-CBT, creative arts techniques have proven to be an effective intervention to support students with anxiety related to these types of events.[19] Pairing these expressive outlets with individual counseling techniques allows students to process their anxiety and develop strategies to manage and reduce their symptoms. Creative arts interventions range from music, drama, and visual arts to dance and photography.[20]

Music

- **Lyric Analysis:** Ask the student to select a song that communicates some part of their experience (the triggering event, the feelings about the event, the anxiety, how the anxiety impacts their life, their hope for reducing anxiety, etc.). Listen to the song together. Consider printing a copy of the lyrics. Allow the student to reflect on the song's lyrics, discussing the lyrics they connect with, and sharing how they would change the lyrics to express themselves more accurately. Listen for opportunities to highlight appropriate coping strategies, challenge faulty thinking, or regulate emotions represented in the lyrics.

- **Life Soundtrack:** Ask the student to create a playlist of songs that represent their life soundtrack. Next have the student share how each song represents part of their story. Ask them if there are songs they *wish* were part of their life soundtrack and allow them to explain why. Create a plan to address what the missing song(s) represent. Suggest that the student use the playlist as a coping strategy when they feel anxious.

- **Anxiety vs. Peace:** Ask the student to select a song that sounds like their anxiety and a song that sounds like peace. Listen to the songs together. Next have the student compare the two songs and identify how parts of each song (music, lyrics, beat, volume, etc.) represent their anxiety and peace. As they differentiate between the two experiences, help them to develop strategies to move toward peace.

15-MINUTE FOCUS
Anxiety Workbook: Tips and Strategies to Manage Anxiety, Build Resilience, and Foster Emotional Well-Being

97

Visual Arts

For these interventions, consider gathering a box of supplies such as construction paper, markers, crayons, glue, stickers, magazines to be cut up, paper plates, craft foam, beads, yarn, paint, and other assorted craft materials.

- **The Mask:** Have the student create a mask. The mask can represent who the anxiety is covering up. The mask can represent who they want to be without their anxiety, or the mask can represent the anxiety itself. As they create their mask, use TF-CBT strategies to educate them about their experience, teach new coping skills, or challenge faulty thinking that may be keeping the mask from allowing them to be who they want to be. As appropriate, develop a plan for managing and reducing their anxiety.

- **Journey T-shirt:** Allow the student to decorate a t-shirt to reflect their life after anxiety. Work together to identify what steps they need to take to manage and reduce their anxiety more effectively.

- **Anxiety Journal:** Students can use a journal to capture their thoughts, feelings, and learning in their journey to overcome their anxiety. Rather than use words in their journal, they can draw or create art to express themselves. If the student is comfortable sharing their journal during individual counseling, ask them to reflect on the meaning of the art included.

- **Getting to the Root of Anxiety:** When we are able to address the root cause that is driving the anxiety, we can alleviate or learn to manage much of the fear that fuels the anxiety. Work with students using CBT techniques to identify the cause(s) of their anxiety. Then allow students to paint rocks representing the cause(s) of their fear about their safety at school. Rocks, much like tree and plant roots, can hold us down. As the student develops strategies to overcome their fears and their anxiety lessens, they can put their rocks in their yard to symbolize that they are no longer allowing the rocks to hold them down.

Photography

Using photography allows the student to explore their experiences with anxiety through various lenses. Students can be directed to take photos that represent safety, anxiety, peace, etc. They could also find pictures that represent these things. Utilizing filters on cell phones can help students understand concepts such as faulty thinking. Exploring the content of the photos as well as the process of taking or finding the pictures creates opportunities for the student to discover awareness concerning their fears about safety at school. For example, if the student shares a picture with other people in it, ask the student to imagine what they may be thinking or feeling about what is happening in the picture, reinforcing the concept that there are multiple ways to view a single event. The student could take a picture of what it means to be brave, or of a person they admire who provided help during a triggering event. Help them identify characteristics they might like to emulate as a positive coping strategy for managing and reducing their anxiety.

A Brave Role Model

(Older Elementary, Middle, High)

Using the **A Brave Role Model Worksheet**, discuss with students the admirable traits they see in others. It can be easier for students to see admirable traits and skills in others. Once they recognize what it means to be brave in someone else, help them to see those qualities in themselves. If there are characteristics they do not have yet, work together to create a plan to develop them. If possible, conduct additional research to see if they have always had that skill. A great follow-up activity is to show the student how their brave hero learned to be brave.

98

15-MINUTE FOCUS
Anxiety Workbook: Tips and Strategies to Manage Anxiety, Build Resilience, and Foster Emotional Well-Being

A Brave Role Model

In the picture frame below, draw a picture of someone you think is brave. Write their name in the name plate.
On the white frame, write what makes them brave.

ROLE MODEL'S NAME

15-MINUTE FOCUS
Anxiety Workbook: Tips and Strategies to Manage Anxiety, Build Resilience, and Foster Emotional Well-Being

99

CHAPTER THREE

Test Anxiety

What is Test Anxiety?

Test anxiety is a specific type of anxiety that occurs in response to the anticipation of, during, or after, academic assessments, tests, or exams. It is tied to the fear of performing poorly on these exams and assessments. It is common among students of all ages, including elementary, middle, and high school students. Test anxiety can have a significant impact on various aspects of a student's life, including their academic performance, emotional well-being, physical health, and social interactions. Recognizing and addressing test anxiety is the first step to helping students manage their stress and succeed academically while maintaining their emotional, physical, and social well-being.

Symptoms of Test Anxiety

Symptoms of test anxiety can range in intensity from mild to severe, and they may vary from one student to another.

Mild Symptoms

- Feeling slightly nervous or uneasy before a test.
- Mild irritability or restlessness.
- Minor difficulty concentrating while studying.
- Occasional self-doubt about performance.

Moderate Symptoms

- Increased worry and nervousness as the test date approaches.
- Physical symptoms like sweaty palms, a slightly elevated heart rate, or butterflies in the stomach.
- More noticeable difficulty focusing on studying.
- Negative self-talk and concern about failure.

100

15-MINUTE FOCUS
Anxiety Workbook: Tips and Strategies to Manage Anxiety, Build Resilience, and Foster Emotional Well-Being

Severe Symptoms

- Intense fear and dread leading up to the test.
- Pronounced physical symptoms such as rapid heartbeat, nausea, trembling, or even panic attacks.
- Significant impairment of concentration and memory during the test.
- Strong feelings of helplessness and catastrophic thinking about failure.
- Avoidance of test-related situations.

Impact of Test Anxiety on Students

Test anxiety can affect students in various ways:

Academically

- Decreased test performance due to impaired cognitive functioning during exams.
- Inaccurate demonstration of knowledge and skills on tests.
- Reduced ability to recall studied information under pressure.
- Lower grades than expected despite adequate preparation.

Emotionally

- Increased levels of stress, worry, and fear.
- Feelings of frustration, disappointment, and self-doubt.
- Lowered self-esteem and self-confidence.
- Potential development or exacerbation of other anxiety-related disorders.

Physically

- Physical symptoms such as headaches, stomachaches, muscle tension, and fatigue.
- Negative impact on overall health and well-being due to chronic stress.

Socially

- Isolation and withdrawal from peers and social activities to focus on studying.
- Difficulty forming new relationships or participating in group activities due to preoccupation with exams.
- Potential strain on existing social relationships due to increased stress and irritability.

15-MINUTE FOCUS
Anxiety Workbook: Tips and Strategies to Manage Anxiety, Build Resilience, and Foster Emotional Well-Being

101

Student Stories

Nora

Nora is a bright and inquisitive 4th-grade white girl with a love for learning. She has a creative and imaginative young spirit, always eager to explore new ideas and concepts. Nora has a kind heart and is often seen helping her classmates with their schoolwork, fostering a friendly and supportive environment in her classroom.

However, Nora has been struggling with a challenging issue: test anxiety. When faced with upcoming exams or assessments, her enthusiasm for learning seems to fade, and she becomes visibly anxious. As the test day approaches, her usual cheerful demeanor transforms into a mixture of uneasiness and self-doubt.

At home, Nora studies diligently, putting in extra effort to prepare for the exams. She is a conscientious student, but the fear of not performing well on the test often overshadows her hard work. Despite her caregivers' encouragement and reassurance, she feels the weight of expectations pressing down on her tiny shoulders.

In the classroom, Nora's test anxiety manifests in various ways. She may fidget, tap her foot, or twirl her hair nervously. When Mrs. McCraw is teaching, she may hesitate to ask questions, fearing her classmates will think she is dumb. Her mind tends to go blank when faced with challenging questions, even if she knows the answers.

On test days, Nora's anxiety intensifies. Her heart races, and her palms become sweaty. She thinks that everyone is watching her, adding to the pressure she feels. Despite her best efforts to focus, she finds it difficult to concentrate and remember the information she studied so diligently. Her teacher recognizes her potential and genuine passion for learning but is concerned about the impact of her test anxiety on her academic progress and emotional well-being.

Darnell

Darnell is 7th-grade African American male who faces the challenges of ADHD along with academic struggles and test anxiety. Darnell is a lively and energetic young boy with a contagious enthusiasm for life. His warm smile and friendly demeanor make him popular among his peers, but his academic difficulties have affected his self-confidence.

Darnell is intelligent and creative; however, he struggles to demonstrate his skills because he faces difficulties in staying focused and organized. He often has trouble following through with tasks and assignments, leading to inconsistent academic performance. His teachers notice that he frequently forgets to complete or turn in assignments and that he sometimes struggles with time management.

Additionally, Darnell's ADHD and academic struggles contribute to test anxiety, making exam days particularly stressful for him. As tests approach, he becomes more anxious and restless, finding it challenging to concentrate and recall the material he studied. His restless energy often leads him to want to move around the classroom during tests, which can be distracting to other students. When he is required to remain in his seat Darnell will tap his pencil, kick his desk, and wiggle in his chair. He can commonly be heard throughout the classroom sighing heavily. There are times, when the anxiety increases, that Darnell gives up and puts his head down on his desk. The pressure to perform well triggers emotional distress, further hindering his ability to showcase his true potential during assessments.

Isabella

11th-grade Latina student Isabella is on a mission to excel in her academics and secure a bright future. With her sights set on attending college, Isabella understands the importance of achieving a high score on the ACT to earn scholarships and access to higher education. However, she is currently facing the significant challenge of test anxiety.

Isabella is a diligent and hardworking student, known among her peers and teachers for her perseverance and passion for learning. She enjoys mathematics and science and hopes to pursue a career in engineering or a related field. With her parents' support and encouragement, Isabella is determined to break barriers and become the first in her family to attend college.

As she prepares for the ACT, the pressure of scoring well and earning scholarships weighs heavily on her shoulders, and it amplifies her feelings of anxiety and stress. She worries that if she does not achieve a certain score, she will not be able to achieve her dreams. In the weeks prior to the ACT, Isabella's test anxiety manifests itself physically, emotionally, and socially. Isabella has enrolled in online test preparation programs to help her study. She spends hours at night taking the practice exams, sacrificing her sleep. She has not noticed that the lack of sleep is starting to impact her health and mood. She often skips meals to study, telling her parents that she does not feel like she can eat because she is so nervous. Isabella does not tell them about the headaches that she has begun having.

Isabella's friends have noticed a shift in her demeanor. Her positive outlook seems to be shadowed by a heaviness. She is not engaging in friendly conversation and has declined invitations for social gatherings with the excuse that she must study. The week before the ACT, Isabella's school counselor is checking in with her students that are preparing for the exam. Isabella snaps at Mrs. Templeton and leaves her office abruptly, very much out of character for her. When Mrs. Templeton tracks her down, she finds Isabella in the restroom in tears. "I'm just so worried about the ACT and I'll never be able to do enough to prepare for it," she cries.

Nora, Darnell, and Isabella are not alone. Many of our students experience test anxiety. Some have mild symptoms that can be addressed with appropriate coping skills while others have more severe signs that will require more interventions.

Consider which you might use to support Nora, Darnell, or Isabella.

15-MINUTE FOCUS
Anxiety Workbook: Tips and Strategies to Manage Anxiety, Build Resilience, and Foster Emotional Well-Being

103

Managing Test Anxiety

ELEMENTARY, MIDDLE, HIGH

LESSON LENGTH	25-40 minutes
OBJECTIVES	• Students will define test anxiety. • Students will identify 2–3 appropriate coping strategies to manage test anxiety.
MATERIALS	• Paper • Colored pencils, markers, or crayons • Coping Skills for Test Anxiety Handout

3 MINUTES — Introduction

- Greet students and share the objectives for the lesson.

5-10 MINUTES — What is Test Anxiety?

- Ask students if they know what test anxiety is and allow several students to share if they have ever felt nervous or worried before a test.

    *Test anxiety is a type of anxiety that is **specific to taking tests**. It is a feeling of nervousness or worry that can occur before, during, or after a test. It comes from a fear of performing poorly on tests and assessments.*

    There may be different reasons we are afraid of failing a test.

- Ask students to suggest reasons why a student might fear failing a test. Possible responses could include getting in trouble with the teacher, getting in trouble with caregivers, getting a bad grade, letting themselves down, needing a good grade to be able to do something special (play on a sports team, get into a school club, get a driver's license, go to college, etc.), or others will judge or make fun of them.

- Reinforce that knowing why we are afraid of failing a test will help us to control and reduce test anxiety.

- Allow students to suggest how test anxiety impacts us. Reinforce answers such as: reduces concentration, memory recall, and performance and leads to a negative self-concept.

104

15-MINUTE FOCUS
Anxiety Workbook: Tips and Strategies to Manage Anxiety, Build Resilience, and Foster Emotional Well-Being

What Does Test Anxiety Look Like?

- Distribute the **paper** and **colored pencils, markers, or crayons**. Depending on the age and number of students, adjust this activity. Divide students into partners or groups of three.
- Ask students to identify symptoms of test anxiety in their group. If you have delivered the classroom lesson on symptoms of general anxiety, remind the students of the symptoms they learned then.
- **Elementary School Students:**
  - They can draw a picture of a student and label the symptoms, write a description of a student experiencing symptoms of test anxiety, or simply list the symptoms on a piece of paper.

  - When students have generated their symptoms, ask each group to share with the class.

- **Middle School Students:**
  - Students can draw a picture of a student and label the symptoms, write a description of a student experiencing symptoms, or create a short skit of a student meeting with the school counselor describing their symptoms of test anxiety.

  - When students have generated their symptoms, ask each group to share with the class.

- **High School Students:**
  - Students can write a description of a student experiencing symptoms or create a short skit of a student meeting with the school counselor and describing their symptoms of test anxiety.

  - When students have generated their symptoms, ask each group to share with the class.

Coping Strategies for Test Anxiety

- Explain that Coping Strategies are actions that we can take to reduce our test anxiety.

  When we use these consistently, they will help us to manage the anxiety we feel associated with tests and assessments.

- Distribute **Coping Skills for Test Anxiety Handout** to students.
- **Elementary School Students:**
  - Ask students to review the different strategies and offer instructions for how to

15-MINUTE FOCUS
Anxiety Workbook: Tips and Strategies to Manage Anxiety, Build Resilience, and Foster Emotional Well-Being

105

use them. For example, on Square Breathing, ask a student to volunteer to show the class how to draw the square in front of them while they breathe in and breath out. Allow students to ask about coping skills they may not understand.

- **Middle and High School Students:**
  - In the same groups, ask to review the different strategies. Select two or three that they will demonstrate to the class how to use (having back-ups ready in case another group selects their first choice). The group will also choose a strategy that they are unfamiliar with or want to know more about.

  - When students are ready, each group will demonstrate their chosen coping skill. Following the demonstration, each group will share the strategy they would like to learn more about. The facilitator or another student(s) can offer further instruction or clarification.

  - As time allows, encourage students to categorize the coping skills into groups according to when they will be most effective: Before the test/assessment, during the test/assessment, or after the test/assessment.

Wrap Up & Assessment

- Review the definition of test anxiety.
- Ask students to hold up two fingers if they can think of two coping skills they can use if they feel test anxiety.
- Encourage the students to keep the worksheet as a reminder that they have the tools to manage and reduce test anxiety.

106

15-MINUTE FOCUS
Anxiety Workbook: Tips and Strategies to Manage Anxiety, Build Resilience, and Foster Emotional Well-Being

Coping Skills for Test Anxiety

Deep Breathing

Get Plenty of Restful Sleep

REPLACE NEGATIVE THOUGHTS WITH POSITIVE THOUGHTS

Eat Healthy Meals

PRACTICE PROGRESSIVE MUSCLE RELAXATION

CREATE A TEST DAY MANTRA, CHANT, OR CHEER, AND REPEAT IT TO YOURSELF ON TEST DAY

PRACTICE MINDFULNESS

Use Positive Language Toward Yourself

Prepare for School the Night Before the Test

STRETCH AND EXERCISE

Visualize Performing Well on the Test

Take Practice Tests

Begin Studying Several Days Before the Test

Ask Questions If You Are Not Sure About the Information for the Test

Plan To Do Something You Enjoy After The Test

Talk to Your School Counselor

15-MINUTE FOCUS
Anxiety Workbook: Tips and Strategies to Manage Anxiety, Build Resilience, and Foster Emotional Well-Being

107

Test Anxiety Skit

(Older Elementary, Middle, High)

Performing a skit provides students involved in the production as well as the audience an opportunity to learn and reinforce knowledge and skills about test anxiety. This short skit could be used as part of school-wide test preparation activities or as an educational strategy for older students performing for younger students.

This script can be found in the Downloadable Resources.

Note: To help drive this activity home, you can have students write the skit in their own voice. How would they help encourage a friend who has test anxiety?

The Test Tackle Trio

Characters

- Alex — Middle school student with test anxiety.
- Maya — Alex's best friend and a confident test-taker.
- Mr. Davis — The wise and supportive school counselor.
- Lily — Another student who has experienced test anxiety before and overcome it.

Setting

School library, where Alex and Maya are studying for an upcoming test.

SCENE 1: THE LIBRARY

(Maya and Alex are sitting at a table, books scattered around them.)

Maya: *(enthusiastically)* Okay, Alex, you've got this! We just have to review these last few chapters, and you'll be ready for the test.

Alex: *(nervously)* I hope so, Maya. I'm so nervous about it! I always get so stressed before tests.

Maya: Don't worry, Alex. You're smart. You always have the right answers when Mrs. Long calls on you in class.

Alex: That's different. Answering questions in class is not a test. Something just happens when a teacher hands me a test. My mind goes blank. My heart starts pounding and I start sweating. Then I can't think about anything other than the fact that I can't remember anything, and I am going to fail! *(Alex tosses his paper on the table, looks down, and sighs loudly.)*

Maya: But you know you have studied because we are studying together. So, you have the right answers in your head. Don't you think you could just take a deep breath or something and refocus?

Alex: I don't know what will work. I just wish I didn't have to take tests. If I could do a project or write a paper, it would be so much better.

108

15-MINUTE FOCUS
Anxiety Workbook: Tips and Strategies to Manage Anxiety, Build Resilience, and Foster Emotional Well-Being

Maya: Have you talked to Mrs. Long about this? Or maybe even Mr. Davis, the school counselor? I wonder if they could help you.

Alex: No. Man, it is embarrassing! I should be able to figure it out. I haven't always felt this way when it comes to tests. I just don't know what to do.

Maya: Well, I do. Let's go talk to Mr. Davis. He is always saying he's here to help us with things like this. *(Maya starts gathering their books and notes.)*

SCENE 2: MR. DAVIS'S OFFICE

(Alex and Maya approach Mr. Davis, the school counselor.)

Mr. Davis: *(smiling)* Hello, Alex, Maya. What brings you here today?

Maya: Hi, Mr. Davis. Alex is feeling anxious about the test, and we were hoping you could give us some advice.

Mr. Davis: Of course! Alex, I imagine that makes preparing for your tests pretty difficult. Test anxiety is a form of anxiety that is tied to worrying about our performance on tests, exams, state assessments, those kinds of things. It is based on fear about failing those tests. Test anxiety is common.

Alex: *(surprised)* It is. Other kids probably deal with this too.

Mr. Davis: Yes sir—and there are ways to manage it. You've already taken the first step.

Maya: What's the first step?

Mr. Davis: It is important to study and review the material covered on the test well before the test, just like you're doing now.

Alex: *(looking worried)* I've been studying, but I still can't shake this feeling of dread.

Maya: That's okay, Alex. I bet Mr. Davis has more tips.

Mr. Davis: One of the things that you and I can do together, Alex, is explore what's making you worry about failing tests. If we can figure out what's behind the fear of failure, then we can work on resolving it. But in the meantime, when you start to have that feeling of dread you mentioned, try some deep breathing. Take a couple of slow breaths in through your nose, hold them for a moment, and then breathe out slowly through your mouth. That kind of breathing will help your brain slow down so that you can refocus on the test rather than the worry about the test. Want to take some practice deep breaths together?

(Mr. Davis, Alex, and Maya take several deep breaths together.)

Alex: *(sounding a little hopeful)* That might help.

Mr. Davis: Another strategy is mindfulness.

15-MINUTE FOCUS
Anxiety Workbook: Tips and Strategies to Manage Anxiety, Build Resilience, and Foster Emotional Well-Being

109

Maya: What is mindfulness?

Mr. Davis: Mindfulness is the act of being present in the moment. Using your senses to notice all the things around you. What do you see, hear, smell, taste, and feel? Paying attention to what is happening around you sort of distracts your brain from worrying. It gives you a chance to break that cycle of worrying that happens with anxiety.

Maya: Oh, I think I had a teacher that did that with us before a test once. She had a metal bowl that made a cool sound.

Mr. Davis: There are a lot of tools that can be used to help us practice mindfulness. But you can also just do it by paying attention to what is around you. That may be a better approach for you to use during a test, Alex, so you don't disturb other students.

Alex: Yeah.

Maya: Or maybe we can get Mrs. Long to do it with the whole class like my other teacher did.

Alex: These are good ideas, Mr. Davis. I don't know if my test anxiety will go away before our next test, but at least I have a couple of things to do if it gets bad again. Maya, I think I'm ready to go tackle that next chapter. Thanks, Mr. Davis. *(Maya and Alex head back to the library.)*

SCENE 3: THE LIBRARY

(After receiving advice from Mr. Davis, Alex and Maya continue studying.)

Maya: All right, Alex, Mr. Davis said deep breathing can calm your nerves. Let's try it.

(They take deep breaths together.)

Maya: See? It helps to relax, right?

Alex: *(feeling a bit better)* Yeah, it does. Thanks, Maya.

(As Maya and Alex are practicing their breathing Lily walks over to them in the library.)

Lily: Hey, guys. Are you getting ready for the test tomorrow?

Alex: *(nervously)* I'm trying but I always get so anxious before tests. We talked to Mr. Davis earlier. I think I have test anxiety.

Lily: *(sympathetic)* I used to feel that way too until I found something that really works for me. Whenever I start to feel anxious, I visualize myself doing well on the test, and it helps me feel more confident.

Alex: How does that work? You just imagine you get an A on the test?

Lily: Well, it's a little more than that. I close my eyes and I see myself calmly reading the test, answering the questions confidently, and notice that I am focused while I am taking the test. Then, of course, I do see the good grade at the end.

Maya: That's a great idea, Lily!

Alex: Just picturing that in your head makes you feel calmer?

Lily: It really does. You would be surprised how visualizing yourself being successful at something you are nervous about can help you to find confidence. It is like doing a trial run in your head where you are in charge. So, of course, you get to do it right! Even though it's in my head, the feeling of success is real. And it does help.

Alex: It sounds a little bit crazy, but it just might work. I think I might be ready for this test tomorrow! *(He smiles at Maya and Lily.)*

SCENE 4: THE LIBRARY

(The next day, the three friends gather in the library after taking the test.)

Alex: *(looking relieved)* I can't believe it. I actually feel pretty good about the test!

Maya: That's amazing, Alex! I knew you could do it!

Lily: See, Alex? You had it in you all along. And remember, even if things didn't go perfectly, it's okay. Tests don't define who we are.

Mr. Davis: *(entering the library)* You're absolutely right, Lily. Tests are just one measure of your abilities. The most important thing is that you gave it your best effort.

Alex: Yeah, I feel like I have a whole toolbox of coping skills now. I will schedule an appointment with you so we can work on the cause of my test anxiety too. Then I bet I won't even have to use those tools as much.

Maya: *(grateful)* Thanks, Mr. Davis. Your advice really helped us all.

Lily: *(smiling)* And we're the Test Tackle Trio!

(They all laugh together.)

[The End]

Questions for Further Discussion

- What kind of student is Alex? Did he get test anxiety because he wasn't smart?
- What were some of the symptoms of Alex's test anxiety? Have you ever experienced test anxiety? What were some of your symptoms?
- What steps did Alex take to address his test anxiety that showed courage? Who are some trusted people you could talk to if you experience test anxiety?
- What were some of the coping strategies that Alex learned to help manage his anxiety? Have you used these coping strategies before? Were they helpful? What other coping strategies have you found to be helpful in managing anxiety?

15-MINUTE FOCUS
Anxiety Workbook: Tips and Strategies to Manage Anxiety, Build Resilience, and Foster Emotional Well-Being

111

Test Anxiety Awareness Social Media Campaign

(High)

Utilizing social media, a class, club, or small group can produce and distribute a public service campaign to educate their fellow students on test anxiety and promote appropriate coping skills. This can be done in conjunction with ACT/SAT testing, final exams, or state assessments.

TikTok Script: "Beat the Test Anxiety Challenge"

OPENING SCENE

Introduce the campaign with a catchy tune and vibrant visuals.

Text Overlay: "Hey High Schoolers!   Let's Tackle Test Anxiety Together!   #BeatTheTestAnxiety #CopingSkills"

SCENE 1

Image/Video: Show a high school student looking stressed while studying with piles of books and papers around them.

Voiceover: "Exams got you feeling overwhelmed? You're not alone! We've got some coping skills to help you ace those tests without anxiety."

SCENE 2

Image/Video: Transition to a classroom setting with a teacher handing out test papers.

Text Overlay: "Step 1: Understand test anxiety"

Voiceover: "To beat it, you gotta know it! Test anxiety is stress before or during exams. Let's break it down!"

SCENE 3

Image/Video: Present animated graphics explaining the symptoms of test anxiety (sweating, racing heart, negative thoughts, etc.).

Voiceover: "Recognize these symptoms? It's all-natural, but we've got ways to cope!"

SCENE 4

Image/Video: Transition to a student taking deep breaths and practicing mindfulness.

Text Overlay: "Step 2: Coping Skills"

Voiceover: "Time to equip yourself with powerful coping skills! Ready?"

112

15-MINUTE FOCUS
Anxiety Workbook: Tips and Strategies to Manage Anxiety, Build Resilience, and Foster Emotional Well-Being

SCENE 5

Image/Video: Show different coping strategies being demonstrated by students: Deep Breathing exercises, Positive Self-talk, Visualization Techniques, Taking Study Breaks, Seeking Support from Friends and Family

Voiceover: "These coping skills will help you stay calm and focused during the test!"

SCENE 6

Image/Video: Highlight a student confidently taking a test with a smile on their face.

Text Overlay: "Step 3: Ace that Test!   "

Voiceover: "You're all set! Now, go and slay that test like a champ! You got this!"

CLOSING SCENE

Image/Video: Gather a group of students cheering and celebrating together.

Text Overlay: "Join the #BeatTheTestAnxiety Challenge! Share your coping skills and support your peers!   "

Voiceover: "Don't forget to share your coping strategies with others and support each other. Together, we'll conquer test anxiety!"

Text Overlay: Show the campaign hashtag: "#BeatTheTestAnxiety"

Text Overlay: "Stay tuned for more tips and tricks! Let's thrive together!   "

Voiceover: "Follow us for more tips to ace those tests and keep stress at bay! You're not alone in this journey!"

END

Follow-Up Social Media Campaign

- Utilize short video clips, infographics, and relatable memes to share test anxiety facts, coping strategies, and success stories.
- Create a dedicated hashtag (#BeatTheTestAnxiety) for students to share their experiences and coping techniques with each other.
- Share motivational quotes and positive affirmations to boost students' confidence.
- Remind students of the mental health resources available at school and in the community.
- Collaborate with school counselors or mental health professionals to host live Q&A sessions or webinars where students can ask questions and receive guidance on managing test anxiety.
- Remember to create content that is engaging, relatable, and positive to foster a supportive online community for high school students dealing with test anxiety.

Classroom Accommodations

Creating a supportive and comfortable learning environment can go a long way in reducing the stress that students experiencing test anxiety feel. It can also provide them an opportunity to demonstrate a more authentic mastery of academic content.

Remember that each student is unique, and the accommodations should be tailored to their specific needs. Engage the student, caregiver, school counselor and/or school social worker to identify helpful accommodations.

When determining the accommodations to provide to students, it is important to consider allowable accommodations for assessments. Most teacher-made tests allow for flexibility in structure and method of delivery. However, many state-mandated assessments have strict guidelines for administration. Even with the support of 504 Accommodation Plans or IEPs, some accommodations may not be available to students. Allowing students to use accommodations in preparation for an assessment that will not permit them to use those same accommodations will increase their anxiety. Keeping this in mind when selecting accommodation supports for students with test anxiety will set them up for success. Consult with your school testing coordinator to identify allowable accommodations.

- **Flexible Testing Environment:** Allow the student to take tests in a separate, quiet, and less intimidating area, away from the usual classroom setting. This can help reduce distractions and promote a sense of calm.
- **Flexible Seating:** Allow the student to choose where they sit during the test to create a comfortable and less stressful environment.
- **Use of Noise-Canceling Headphones:** Allow students to use noise-canceling headphones to block out external distractions during the test.
- **Assistive Technology:** Allow the use of assistive technology tools, such as word processors or speech-to-text software, for students who may struggle with handwriting or organizing thoughts on paper.
- **Extended Time:** Offer extra time for the student to complete tests, ensuring they do not feel rushed or pressured.
- **Breaks:** Allow short breaks during the test to help the student relax and refocus their thoughts.
- **Chunking:** Break longer tests into smaller, manageable sections. This allows the student to focus on one part at a time, reducing the feeling of being overwhelmed.
- **Encourage Positive Self-Talk:** Teach the student strategies to cope with anxiety, such as positive self-talk and mindfulness exercises.
- **Practice Tests:** Offer practice tests before the actual test to familiarize the student with the format and reduce anxiety.
- **Modeling and Examples:** Use sample problems or questions that are similar to those on the test to demonstrate problem-solving techniques and test-taking strategies.
- **Alternative Assessment:** Consider using alternative assessment methods, such as projects, presentations, or open-book tests, which can be less anxiety-provoking for some students.
- **Positive Reinforcement:** Provide positive reinforcement and praise for effort and improvement rather than solely focusing on grades.
- **Encourage Test-Taking Strategies:** Teach effective test-taking strategies, such as skimming through the test first, answering easier questions first, and managing time wisely.

- **Regular Check-ins:** Have regular check-ins with the student to discuss their concerns and feelings about tests and provide reassurance and support.
- **Incorporate Mindful Activities:** Integrate mindful activities and exercises into the daily routine to reduce overall stress levels.

Individual Counseling Interventions for Students Experiencing Test Anxiety

In addition to the individual counseling interventions for general anxiety, the following activities and worksheets can be used with individual students to help them learn about test anxiety, understand their own experiences with test anxiety, identify strategies to better manage their test anxiety, and practice coping skills to reduce their test anxiety. Instructions and probing questions to help students process the content of the activity are suggested below. Check the chart in the Table of Contents to identify activities for the grade level representing your student.

Test Anxiety Road Trip

(Elementary, Middle, High)

Test anxiety is grounded in fear of failing tests, exams, or assessments. Helping students identify what is driving these fears is a powerful step in managing and reducing the test anxiety they experience. The following questions may help the student identify the root cause of the fear fueling the test anxiety:

"What is the worst that will happen if you fail a test?"

"What is your biggest worry about failing a test?"

"What are you afraid will happen if you fail a test?"

As the student shares their responses, help them narrow down to a primary fear associated with failing a test. Then, using the **Test Anxiety Road Trip Worksheet**, tell the student you are going to go on a Test Anxiety Road Trip to explore what is driving their test anxiety. Have the student write what is driving their fear of failure on the car at the start of the road trip.

Note: If the student discloses a fear associated with a physical or emotional threat to their safety, or issues that fall under mandated reporting laws, follow your district's policies for supporting students in those circumstances. The test anxiety can be revisited once the student's safety has been addressed.

15-MINUTE FOCUS
Anxiety Workbook: Tips and Strategies to Manage Anxiety, Build Resilience, and Foster Emotional Well-Being

115

Process with the student what might actually happen if their fear were to be realized. At each road sign, have the student record the possible outcomes. If the student is afraid that they will be grounded for failing a test, at the first road sign, ask them what happens if they get grounded. Do they miss out on an activity? Do they lose phone/ internet privileges? Work through several different possible outcomes associated with their realized fear. Challenge any cognitive distortions such as catastrophic or all-or-nothing thinking. Helping the student see that they will survive their worst fear can reduce its power to trigger significant anxiety.

Reinforce coping skills and test-taking strategies the student can use to manage their anxiety and prepare for the tests.

Coping Skills for Test Anxiety

(Elementary, Middle, High)

Helping students identify strategies and actions they can take to manage and reduce their test anxiety will give them a sense of agency and control. The **Coping Skills for Test Anxiety Worksheet** can be used in classroom lessons and with individual students. Spend time discussing the various strategies ensuring the student understands how to use each of the coping skills appropriately. Practicing the skills together is a fun way to model them for the student and allows you to assess their mastery.

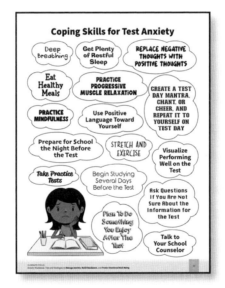

116

15-MINUTE FOCUS
Anxiety Workbook: Tips and Strategies to Manage Anxiety, Build Resilience, and Foster Emotional Well-Being

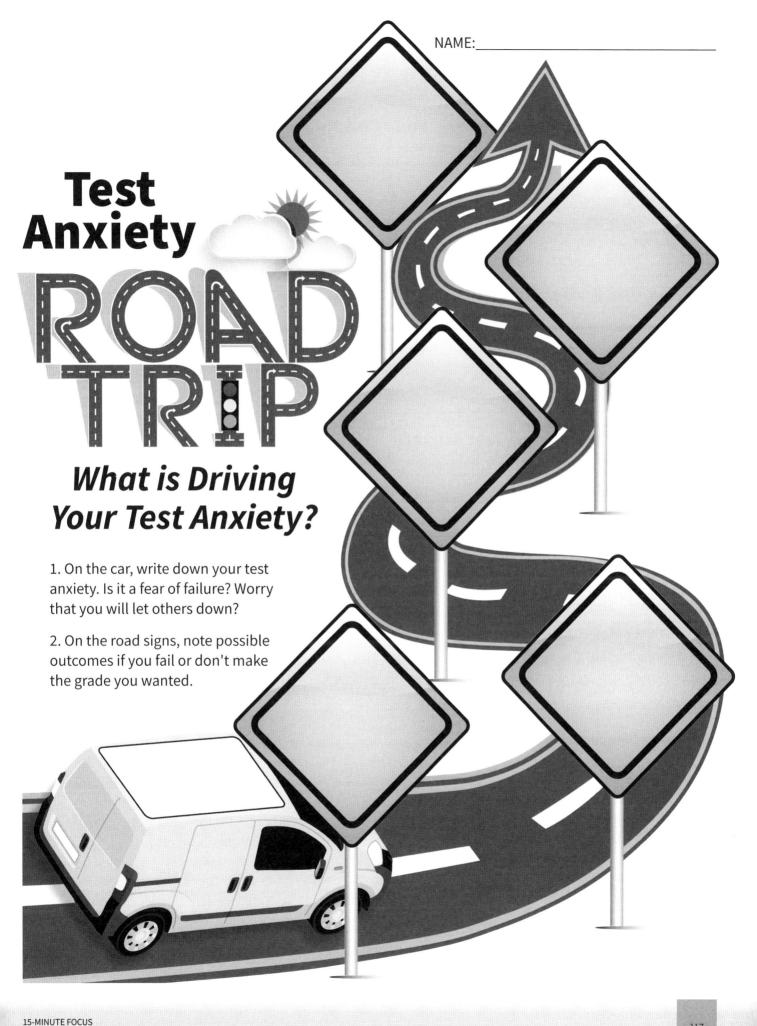

Test Anxiety

ROAD TRIP

What is Driving Your Test Anxiety?

1. On the car, write down your test anxiety. Is it a fear of failure? Worry that you will let others down?

2. On the road signs, note possible outcomes if you fail or don't make the grade you wanted.

15-MINUTE FOCUS
Anxiety Workbook: Tips and Strategies to Manage Anxiety, Build Resilience, and Foster Emotional Well-Being

117

Caregiver Information on Test Anxiety

Understanding and Supporting Your Child's Test Anxiety

As caregivers, we know that our children's education involves more than just academic learning; it also includes navigating the emotional challenges that can arise during their school journey. One common hurdle many students face is test anxiety. Test anxiety is a feeling of nervousness and worry that can occur before, during, or after taking a test. It is essential for caregivers to recognize the signs and learn how to support their children in managing this stress.

What is Test Anxiety?

Test anxiety is an emotional response to the pressure of exams or assessments. It can manifest differently in students of various age groups. Younger children may have difficulty expressing their feelings, while older ones might internalize their stress. Understanding the signs of test anxiety can help caregivers offer appropriate assistance.

Common Symptoms of Test Anxiety

Elementary School Students

- Complaining of stomachaches or headaches on test days.
- Exhibiting restlessness or fidgeting.
- Avoiding talking about tests or school.
- Becoming more clingy or seeking excessive reassurance.

Middle School Students

- Feeling irritable or moody before tests.
- Having trouble sleeping the night before an exam.
- Overthinking about past test performance.
- Becoming more withdrawn or avoiding friends.

High School Students

- Experiencing a rapid heartbeat or shortness of breath during tests.
- Feeling overwhelmed and unable to concentrate.
- Engaging in negative self-talk about their abilities.
- Engaging in avoidance behaviors, like skipping school or procrastinating.

Strategies to Support Your Child

Elementary School Students

- **Encourage a positive attitude toward learning:** Emphasize effort and progress rather than just the final grades.

- **Establish a consistent study routine:** Help your child create a study schedule that includes short breaks and time for fun activities.
- **Offer rewards and incentives:** Motivate your child with small rewards after completing study sessions or tests.

Middle School Students

- **Teach relaxation techniques:** Breathing exercises and mindfulness can help manage stress.
- **Promote Healthy Habits:** Ensure your child gets enough sleep, eats well, and exercises regularly.
- **Set Realistic Goals:** Encourage them to set achievable objectives for their studies.

High School Students

- **Assist with time management:** Help your child plan their study schedule and avoid last-minute cramming.
- **Encourage seeking help:** Remind them that it is okay to ask teachers for assistance when needed.
- **Provide perspective:** Share your experiences with overcoming challenges and learning from mistakes.

Discussion Starters for Conversations with Children

Many children are afraid to talk about their feelings of anxiety. Having a trusted adult initiate the conversation can actually reduce their anxiety. The most effective discussions take place when the child is feeling calm and secure in a comfortable environment. Here are some questions that can help you start conversations with your child about their anxiety:

Elementary School Students

- "How do you feel about taking tests or quizzes?"
- "What can I do to help you feel less stressed about school?"

Middle School Students

- "Are there any subjects or topics that make you feel particularly anxious?"
- "Let's create a study plan together to make things more manageable."
- "What will happen if you do not do well on this test?"

High School Students

- "How do you prepare for tests, and do you feel it's effective?"
- "If you feel overwhelmed, what can I do to support you?"
- "It's normal to feel nervous but remember that you have the ability to overcome challenges. Do you remember another time you overcame a challenge?"

As caregivers, our support plays a significant role in helping our children build resilience and cope with test anxiety. By understanding their feelings and offering appropriate strategies, we can create a positive and nurturing environment for their academic growth and emotional well-being. If your student needs additional assistance, please reach out to the school counselor for support.

15-MINUTE FOCUS
Anxiety Workbook: Tips and Strategies to Manage Anxiety, Build Resilience, and Foster Emotional Well-Being

119

Let's Check-in with Our Students

How did the staff at our students' school support them?

Nora

Mrs. McCraw ensures that the classroom environment remains supportive and nurturing, creating a safe space where students, including Nora, feel comfortable seeking help and expressing their concerns. Nora's caregivers and teacher work together to find strategies to help alleviate her test anxiety. They encourage her to use deep breathing to calm her nerves and visualization exercises to build her confidence before and during exams. Mrs. McCraw has also employed an alternative assessment method in one subject to assess Nora's true abilities, allowing her to demonstrate her knowledge and skills without the paralyzing pressure of the traditional test.

With a compassionate and supportive community around her, Nora begins to gradually overcome her test anxiety. She learns to trust in her abilities and recognizes that making mistakes is a natural part of the learning process. As she continues to grow academically and emotionally, Nora discovers that tests are not a measure of her worth, but rather a chance to show what she has learned and how she continues to improve each day.

Darnell

Darnell has recognized that he has a strong support system at school and home. His teachers and parents work together to provide him with accommodations and strategies to manage his ADHD and test anxiety. They understand the importance of breaking down tasks into smaller, manageable steps, providing visual aids, and incorporating interactive learning techniques to keep him engaged.

Darnell's family and teachers also emphasize the development of coping skills to address test anxiety. They encourage relaxation techniques, such as deep breathing exercises and mindfulness practices, to help him stay calm and focused during exams. Darnell is beginning to believe that, with the right interventions and nurturing environment, he can overcome his challenges and build on his unique strengths to find success.

Isabella

Recognizing that support is essential for overcoming her test anxiety, Isabella turns to her school counselor, teachers, and friends for guidance and encouragement. She engages in study groups, where she can discuss concepts, share tips, and provide support to others facing the same challenges. Isabella seeks various strategies to stay focused and calm during her study sessions. She creates a structured study schedule, setting aside dedicated time each day to review the test material, practice problems, and take practice tests. Isabella is aware that consistent practice will build her confidence and improve her performance.

Isabella also takes care of her physical and mental well-being to manage test anxiety. Regular exercise, yoga, and mindfulness practices help her relax and maintain a positive mindset. She ensures she gets enough rest and eats nutritious meals to stay energized and focused. Despite the obstacles and uncertainties, Isabella's motivation to succeed remains unwavering. She knows that overcoming test anxiety is crucial to achieving her goals, and she refuses to let fear hinder her progress. With her determination, resilience, and a strong support system, Isabella is confident that she will rise above her test anxiety and achieve the results she desires on the ACT.

CHAPTER FOUR

Social Anxiety

What is Social Anxiety?

Social anxiety is an anxiety disorder characterized by an intense fear of social situations and interactions. It can affect students of all ages. Those who suffer with social anxiety worry about being judged, embarrassed, or humiliated in front of others, leading them to avoid many social situations, such as meeting new people, eating or drinking with others, and performing in front of any size audience. Social anxiety is distinct from general anxiety in that it specifically pertains to social interactions and situations that trigger an excessive and often irrational fear of negative evaluation or rejection by others.

Symptoms of Social Anxiety

Symptoms of social anxiety can vary in intensity from mild to severe, and they may manifest differently in students:

Mild Symptoms

- Slight discomfort or nervousness in social situations.
- Reluctance to participate in class discussions or group activities.
- Mild self-consciousness and concern about others' opinions.

Moderate Symptoms

- Heightened anxiety and self-consciousness in social settings.
- Avoidance of situations where the student may be the center of attention.
- Increased physical symptoms like blushing, trembling, or sweating.
- Difficulty making eye contact or speaking up in public.

Severe Symptoms

- Intense fear of public speaking or performing in front of others.
- Extreme avoidance of social situations, even those necessary for academic or social engagement.
- Physical symptoms such as panic attacks, rapid heartbeat, nausea, and shaking.
- Profound distress and impaired functioning in daily life.

15-MINUTE FOCUS
Anxiety Workbook: Tips and Strategies to Manage Anxiety, Build Resilience, and Foster Emotional Well-Being

121

Impact of Social Anxiety on Students

Social anxiety can impact students in various ways:

Academically

- Reluctance or refusal to participate in class discussions and presentations.
- Difficulty asking questions or seeking help from teachers.
- Lowered academic performance due to avoidance of group projects or oral exams.

Emotionally

- Intense feelings of fear, embarrassment, and self-consciousness.
- Low self-esteem and negative self-image.
- Increased stress and emotional distress.

Physically

- Headaches, stomachaches, muscle tension, and fatigue.
- Impact on overall well-being due to chronic stress.

Socially

- Isolation and difficulty forming and maintaining friendships.
- Avoidance of social events and activities.
- Strain on existing relationships due to avoidance behaviors.

Role of Social Media on Social Anxiety

The creation and advancement of social media has played a significant role in our students' experiences. Students use social media platforms to access information and each other. With a keystroke, they can reach out to hundreds and thousands of people. And all of those people can reach back out to them. People post pictures of their best moments, filtered and designed to hide any imperfections. This creates unrealistic expectations for our students that they then criticize themselves for not meeting. Others hide behind their screens while attacking students with lies or exposing their vulnerabilities. Gossip can spread throughout a school in mere minutes.

Although social media has shown us the best of humanity, the images of our worst moments seem to persist far longer. Engagement in social media can exacerbate distress for some students. Evidence points to positive correlation between students who are victims of cyberbullying and those experiencing social anxiety.[21]

Social media can contribute to social anxiety by:

- Creating unrealistic comparisons with others' lives, leading to feelings of inadequacy.
- Amplifying the fear of judgment and scrutiny from peers.
- Facilitating cyberbullying and negative online interactions.
- Fostering a sense of constant connectivity and performance pressure.

It is important for educators, parents, and caregivers to recognize the signs of social anxiety in students and provide appropriate support. Creating a supportive and understanding environment, along with teaching healthy social media habits, can also play a crucial role in mitigating the impact of social anxiety on students.

Student Stories

Amelia

Amelia is an 8-year-old 2nd grade student with social anxiety, living in a diverse suburban community. Her Chinese American parents, both hardworking professionals, place a high value on academic achievements and strive to support their only child in every way they can. At home, Amelia displays several symptoms of social anxiety. She becomes visibly nervous and apprehensive when her parents invite guests over. She tends to retreat to her room, avoiding social interactions even with close relatives. Amelia rarely participates in extracurricular activities or playdates, preferring to stay home where she feels more secure and in control. When her parents try to gently encourage her to engage with others, she often exhibits signs of distress, such as increased heart rate, stomachaches, and crying.

At school, Amelia's social anxiety is more evident. She finds it challenging to initiate conversations with her classmates and is fearful of being judged or criticized. During class activities that involve group work, she becomes extremely anxious and tries to blend into the background to avoid attention. Amelia rarely raises her hand in class, even when she knows the answer, fearing that her response might be incorrect. Despite being intelligent and capable, she struggles to actively participate in class discussions and often misses out on opportunities to showcase her knowledge and skills. Her grades are starting to reflect her lack of participation, which adds to Amelia's worry.

She tends to spend her lunch alone or with a single close friend she feels comfortable around. Recess and gym class cause her distress because she worries about making mistakes or being rejected by her classmates. Her social anxiety limits her ability to make new friends and develop meaningful connections with her peers. This isolation has led to feelings of loneliness and further exacerbated her anxiety. Amelia frequently experiences intense emotions like worry, fear, and self-doubt. This emotional burden has negatively affected her self-esteem and confidence, making it harder for her to develop a positive self-image.

Jaime

Jaime is a 13-year-old middle school student living in a diverse urban community. They identify as nonbinary and their Hispanic parents are understanding and supportive of their identity, illustrative of valuing strong family ties and communal support. Jaime has been experiencing social anxiety, particularly triggered by engagement on social media. They spend a significant amount of time on various social media platforms, but it becomes a double-edged sword for them. While social media helps them stay connected to friends and peers, it also triggers their anxiety. They often feel overwhelmed by the constant comparison to others, fearing they do not measure up or are not as popular or attractive as their peers. Jaime has also been the target of cyberbullying because of their gender identity. They have not shared these experiences with their parents because Jaime feels a great deal of shame, is not aware of the perpetrator, and does not believe that anything can be done to stop it.

At home, Jaime exhibits several symptoms of social anxiety. They become withdrawn, spending long periods of time alone in their room, and avoiding family gatherings or social events with relatives. Their parents notice Jaime has struggled to express their feelings, which has begun limiting their once-open communication. They may experience headaches, stomachaches, or changes in sleep

15-MINUTE FOCUS
Anxiety Workbook: Tips and Strategies to Manage Anxiety, Build Resilience, and Foster Emotional Well-Being

123

patterns due to the emotional toll of their social anxiety. Jaime experiences heightened emotions like fear, self-doubt, and sadness. The constant comparison on social media contributes to feelings of insecurity, leading to decreased self-esteem and a negative perception of themselves.

When at school, Jaime's social anxiety is heightened, especially in social situations. They feel a strong sense of self-consciousness and worry about being judged or excluded by their classmates. During group activities or class discussions, they find it challenging to voice their opinions or share ideas, fearing ridicule or rejection, which affects their concentration and performance in class. They struggle to focus on assignments and often procrastinate on tasks due to anxiety about meeting expectations or being judged by their peers. Social media also impacts their school experience negatively. Online interactions with classmates can escalate their anxiety as they obsessively check for likes, comments, or mentions, which becomes a source of validation or criticism of their self-worth. Jaime wonders if the cyberbully is someone at their school so they experience increased paranoia, pondering who might be watching them, gathering information for the next post.

Samira

Samira is a 17-year-old female high school student whose family moved to the United States several years ago from Jordan in the Middle East. Her parents value family honor and community and have immersed themselves in a region of an urban area where other relatives and friends from Jordan have also immigrated. Samira is proud of her heritage, but she often feels conflicted between societal expectations and her personal aspirations to adopt more American cultural practices. This inner struggle contributes to the social anxiety Samira experiences.

Samira began exhibiting symptoms of social anxiety shortly after her family settled in their new home, particularly during situations that involve extended family gatherings or community events. She becomes extremely nervous and self-conscious, fearing that she may say or do something to bring shame to her family. This anxiety causes her to withdraw from social interactions, preferring to spend time alone in her room where she feels safer and less likely to face judgment. Her parents, who value close family relationships, encourage her to participate in family gatherings, but Samira's anxiety often leads to physical symptoms like trembling hands, increased heart rate, and difficulty breathing. She struggles to articulate her feelings and thoughts, fearing that she might say something inappropriate or controversial. Samira feels a constant pressure to uphold cultural expectations, leading to internal conflicts between her personal desires and societal norms, which causes Samira to experience fear, shame, and guilt.

At school, Samira's social anxiety manifests during classroom discussions and group projects. She finds it difficult to speak up or share her opinions, fearing judgment by her classmates or teacher. Although she has been a successful student in the past, Samira's fear of participating in class discussions hampers her academic performance.

Samira tends to isolate herself during lunch breaks, preferring to eat alone or stay in the library, avoiding the overwhelming social atmosphere of the cafeteria. Making friends is also a challenge for Samira. She worries that others might misunderstand or judge her cultural background, leading to a sense of isolation and loneliness.

CLASSROOM
LESSON

Building an Inclusive and Accepting Classroom Community to Reduce Social Anxiety

ELEMENTARY

LESSON LENGTH	25 minutes
OBJECTIVES	• Students will demonstrate that social anxiety is a type of anxiety with avoidance behaviors due to fear of judgment from others. • Students will identify two strategies they can employ to build a judgment-free classroom community.
MATERIALS	• Poster board or construction paper • Colored pencils, markers, or crayons

Introduction

- Welcome students and review objectives for the lesson.
- If lessons on anxiety have been delivered previously, ask students to recall information such as the definition of anxiety, what drives anxiety, etc.

What is Social Anxiety?

- Explain to students what social anxiety is.

    Social Anxiety *a type of anxiety that occurs when someone feels anxious and worried about being around people because they are afraid of being judged, made fun of, or embarrassed. They get so worried that they are unable to go out to do things that most people consider pretty typical.*

- Ask students to suggest activities that social anxiety might prevent someone from doing (attending school, extracurricular activities, going to the store, etc.). Allow students to imagine what life would be like if they were afraid of being judged everywhere they went.

15-MINUTE FOCUS
Anxiety Workbook: Tips and Strategies to Manage Anxiety, Build Resilience, and Foster Emotional Well-Being

125

How might someone with social anxiety be impacted at school? With friends?

- Share symptoms of social anxiety:
  - **Mild Symptoms:** Discomfort or nervousness in social situations, reluctance to participate in class discussions or group activities, or mild self-consciousness and concern about others' opinions.

  - **Moderate Symptoms:** Heightened anxiety and self-consciousness in social settings, avoidance of situations where the student may be the center of attention, physical symptoms such as blushing, trembling, or sweating, and difficulty making eye contact or speaking up in public.

  - **Severe Symptoms:** Intense fear of public speaking or performing in front of others, extreme avoidance of social situations (even those necessary for academic or social engagement), physical symptoms such as panic attacks, rapid heartbeat, nausea, and shaking, and profound distress and impaired functioning in daily life.

- Make sure to differentiate between normal anxiety before speaking in front of the class or before a presentation and social anxiety.

  Some nervous feelings are very common. If those nervous feelings make it really difficult for us to complete the task or we are unable to participate in regular activities, then we need to ask for help.

- Explain that there are ways to help someone who has social anxiety.

  Using appropriate coping strategies, talking to a counselor or social worker, or getting support from a doctor are all helpful things we can do when experiencing social anxiety.

- Introduce the next activity by sharing that we can also help when a friend experiences social anxiety.

Building an Inclusive and Supportive Classroom Community

10
MINUTES

- Ask the students to recall why students who experience social anxiety do not want to go out in public? (Fear of being judged, embarrassed, made fun of, etc.)
- Suggest to students that if their classroom was a judgment-free zone it might make students experiencing social anxiety feel safer. Have students brainstorm what a **judgment-free classroom** could look like. Record answers on the board. Consider dividing older elementary students into small groups to brainstorm together.
- After brainstorming, review the suggestions from the class. Try to position each suggestion as a positive action that students can take. For example, be kind to each other, offer help to someone that is having trouble understanding something, or complement each other.

- As students discuss their list, listen for the idea of **inclusion**. If it is not brought up directly, introduce inclusivity.

  Everyone is a valued part of our class. We celebrate our differences. We recognize we all have different strengths, and we use them to help each other. We understand that by supporting each other it makes our whole class a better place for everyone.

- Let the students consider how their previous suggestions support or build an inclusive classroom environment.
- Assist the students in coming to a consensus on 5–7 specific actions to build a supportive and inclusive classroom environment.
- Next, select one of the activities below or use one of your own (or students' suggestion) to demonstrate their commitment to building an inclusive classroom:
  - **Build an Inclusive Billboard:** Divide the class into the same number of groups as the specific actions they identified. Using **poster board or construction paper** and **colored pencils, markers, or crayons,** each group will decorate their section of the billboard with their specific action. Once all of the groups are done, the sections can be posted together to create a billboard announcing that this is a supportive and inclusive community.

  - **Create a Classroom Pledge:** Develop a classroom pledge that incorporates the student-identified actions. Divide the class into the same number of groups as specific actions they generated. Each group will turn their action into a statement reflecting their commitment to support an inclusive classroom. The statements can be combined into a **poster** that every student will sign. An alternative is to post each statement individually after students have signed them.

Wrap Up & Assessment

- Ask students to recall the definition of social anxiety.
- Allow students to identify two of the specific actions they are excited about doing to create an inclusive and supportive classroom.
- Consider following up with students periodically to check-in on their progress implementing their activities. Allow students to ask questions or request help for situations that may have come up in their classroom.

Embracing Diversity to Reduce Social Anxiety

MIDDLE, HIGH

LESSON LENGTH	40 minutes
OBJECTIVES	• Students will demonstrate that social anxiety is a type of anxiety with avoidance behaviors due to fear of judgment from others. • Students will identify two strategies they can employ to build a judgment-free school community.
MATERIALS	• Index cards or sticky notes

5 MINUTES

Introduction

- Welcome students and review objectives for the lesson.
- If lessons on anxiety have been delivered previously, ask students to recall information such as the definition of anxiety, what drives anxiety, etc.

10 MINUTES

What is Social Anxiety?

- Explain to students that social anxiety is.

  Social Anxiety is a type of anxiety that occurs when someone feels anxious and worried about being around people because they are afraid of being judged, made fun of, or embarrassed. They get so worried that they are unable to go out to do things that most people consider pretty typical.

- Ask students to suggest activities that social anxiety might prevent someone from doing (attending school, extracurricular activities, going to the store, etc.). Allow students to imagine what life would be like if they were afraid of being judged everywhere they went.

  How might someone with social anxiety be impacted at school? With friends? At work? On social media?

- Share symptoms of social anxiety:
  - **Mild Symptoms:** Discomfort or nervousness in social situations they do engage in, reluctance to participate in class discussions or group activities, or mild self-consciousness and concern about others' opinions.

15-MINUTE FOCUS
Anxiety Workbook: Tips and Strategies to Manage Anxiety, Build Resilience, and Foster Emotional Well-Being

- **Moderate Symptoms:** Heightened anxiety and self-consciousness in social settings, avoidance of situations where the student may be the center of attention, physical symptoms such as blushing, trembling, or sweating, and difficulty making eye contact or speaking up in public.

- **Severe Symptoms:** Intense fear of public speaking or performing in front of others, extreme avoidance of social situations (even those necessary for academic or social engagement), physical symptoms such as panic attacks, rapid heartbeat, nausea, and shaking, and profound distress and impaired functioning in daily life.

- Make sure to differentiate between normal anxiety before speaking in front of the class or before a presentation and social anxiety.

  Some nervous feelings are very common. If those nervous feelings make it really difficult for us to complete the task or we are unable to participate in regular activities, then we need to ask for help.

- Explain that there are ways to help someone that has social anxiety.

  Using appropriate coping strategies, talking to a counselor or social worker, or getting support from a doctor are all helpful things we can do when we experience social anxiety.

- Introduce the next activity by sharing that we can also help when a friend experiences social anxiety.

Respecting Diversity

- Remind students that the fear of being judged or embarrassed is at the root of social anxiety. One of the ways that we can support students who experience social anxiety is to **create inclusive and supportive environments**. Ask students to suggest reasons why someone might fear being judged. Reinforce answers aligned to concepts of being different, not meeting social, academic, physical, or socioeconomic expectations, etc.

- Prompt students to consider whether their own actions intentionally or unintentionally contribute to a less inclusive and accepting environment. Depending on the suggestions given and developmental level of the students, select one of the activities below to increase awareness and appreciation for diversity.

  - **Find Your Common Ground:** Have students pair up or form small groups. Give each pair/group an **index card or sticky note** and ask them to find at least five things they have in common (e.g., hobbies, interests, favorite movies, etc.). After they have found their common ground, have each pair/group share a few of their similarities with the whole class.

  - **Understanding Stereotypes, and Prejudices:** Lead a discussion about stereotypes and prejudices, explaining their negative impact on individuals and communities. You can use real-life examples to illustrate the consequences of stereotypes and how they can lead to discrimination and exclusion. Allow

15-MINUTE FOCUS
Anxiety Workbook: Tips and Strategies to Manage Anxiety, Build Resilience, and Foster Emotional Well-Being

129

students to share personal experiences as they are comfortable, or they can share observations related to stereotypes and prejudices in general.

- **Empathy Through Storytelling:** Ask the students to gather in a circle and share a personal experience when they felt excluded, different, or misunderstood. Encourage active listening and empathy from their peers during the storytelling process. After each student shares their story, have the rest of the class offer supportive comments or feedback to show understanding and acceptance. Conclude by emphasizing the importance of empathy and actively supporting one another. You can divide the class into smaller groups for this activity.

- **A Day in the Life:** Tell the students that an alien from another planet has arrived at the school. The alien will be attending their school. Divide the class into groups and assign each group different times of the day from before school until after school. Each group should describe what the alien is likely to experience (the good and the not-so-good). After all groups have shared what the alien is likely to experience, facilitate a discussion about what the alien might tell his fellow aliens about being accepted/or not.

An Inclusive and Supportive Environment Starts with Me

- As students have reflected through the previous activities, remind them they have the power to support students who experience social anxiety by contributing to an inclusive and supportive school environment.

- Distribute an **index card** to every student. Instruct them to write the following statement on the front of the card: "**An inclusive and supportive school environment is important because**" and ask them to complete the sentence.

- On the other side of the card students should write: "**To build an inclusive and supportive school environment I will**" and they will complete the sentence identifying one specific action that they will **continue**, one action they will **stop**, and one specific action they will **start** doing.

- As time allows, students can share how they are going to contribute to an inclusive and supportive school environment.

Wrap Up & Assessment

- The index cards can serve as an exit ticket to assess student learning after the lesson. However, consider allowing students to keep their index card as a reminder of their commitment to helping students who experience social anxiety.

- Consider a follow-up or check-in with students to assess how they can contribute to an inclusive and supportive school community. It is a good reminder that it takes time and practice to change behaviors, so encourage those that may acknowledge having challenges. Conducting role plays and "what if" conversations can help students learn to navigate more challenging situations.

130

15-MINUTE FOCUS
Anxiety Workbook: Tips and Strategies to Manage Anxiety, Build Resilience, and Foster Emotional Well-Being

Classroom Accommodations

Because judgment and embarrassment are at the root of social anxiety, affirming students who experience social anxiety for their inherent value will build their self-concept. Normalizing mistakes as a part of the learning process rather than as failures helps to remove the isolation that social anxiety often causes. Remember that each student is unique, and the accommodations should be tailored to their specific needs. Engage the student, caregiver, school counselor and/or school social worker to identify helpful accommodations.

- **Flexible Seating Arrangements:** Allow the student to sit in a location that feels more comfortable for them, such as near the teacher or in a quiet corner away from high-traffic areas.
- **Buddy System:** Pair the student with a supportive classmate who can act as a "buddy" during group activities or free time.
- **Break Cards:** Provide the student with break cards they can discreetly show the teacher when feeling overwhelmed or needing some time alone.
- **Advance Notice of Changes:** Inform the student in advance about any changes to the daily routine or upcoming events to reduce anxiety about the unknown.
- **Signal for Help:** Develop a nonverbal signal (e.g., raising a hand or using a specific object) that the student can use to indicate they need assistance or a break.
- **Small Group Activities:** Organize activities in small groups to reduce the overwhelming feeling of being in a large crowd.
- **Modified Presentations:** Offer alternatives to oral presentations, such as written reports or multimedia projects, to reduce anxiety related to public speaking.
- **Flexible Participation:** Allow the student to participate in class discussions or activities at their comfort level, without pressure to speak or engage beyond their capabilities.
- **Positive Reinforcement:** Recognize and praise the student's efforts to participate or engage in social situations, no matter how small.
- **Teacher Understanding and Patience:** Ensure that other teachers and adults at school are aware of the student's social anxiety and are patient and understanding when the student is hesitant to engage with them.
- **Respect Personal Boundaries:** Teach classmates how to respect the personal space and boundaries of all students. This will benefit the student experiencing social anxiety without bringing specific attention to them.

Individual Counseling Interventions for Students Experiencing Social Anxiety

The following worksheets can be used with individual students to help them learn about social anxiety, understand their own experiences with social anxiety, identify strategies to better manage their social anxiety, and practice coping skills to reduce their social anxiety. Instructions and probing questions to help students process the content of the activity are suggested below.

15-MINUTE FOCUS
Anxiety Workbook: Tips and Strategies to Manage Anxiety, Build Resilience, and Foster Emotional Well-Being

131

Gratitude Journaling

(Elementary, Middle, High)

Research has found that practicing gratitude can increase a person's ability to evaluate situations in a more positive light, which could lead to reduction in feelings of anxiety.[22] Students experiencing social anxiety have difficulty appraising situations without an element of judgment.

Encouraging students of all ages to practice gratitude through writing one or two journal entries (see the **Gratitude Journal**) or keeping a gratitude journal is a positive way to help students reframe their perspectives. If the student is comfortable sharing, allow them to highlight the things that bring them gratitude. Help them to focus on those positive experiences as a strategy to reduce their anxiety. Students can choose from one of the **Gratitude Journal Writing Prompts** or free write about something specific they feel thankful for in their lives on the worksheet. When working with younger elementary students, consider selecting a specific writing prompt and allowing them to draw their response.

Can vs. Should

(Middle, High)

Believing you can do something comes from a place of curiosity and confidence. Believing you should do something comes from a place of judgment. When students feel like they have to do things that they do not want to, or will be judged for doing them, it increases anxiety. Helping students reframe those tasks to see them from a place of curiosity and control can lessen the anxiety they associate with them. When students learn to approach themselves with "can" instead of "should" they will reduce the internal judgment they feel that intensifies their social anxiety.

Lead the middle or high school student through the activity using the **Can vs. Should Worksheet**, asking them to identify something they feel like they *should* do and something they feel like they *can* do. Explore how they feel about each activity. Encourage them to shift their perspective to being curious, even when doing something they have to do like homework, projects, etc. Some students may need to talk through reframing several examples to practice this skill.

I Am Enough

(Middle, High)

Give the **I Am Enough Coloring Sheet** to any student during an individual session. Because social anxiety is rooted in judgment, helping students to identify their strengths and talents can help them build their self-confidence and self-concept. Both are strong protective factors against social anxiety. The coloring sheet is a reminder that, just as they are, they are enough.

Gratitude Journal

Identifying people, things, and opportunities that produce feelings of gratitude is a proven strategy for reducing social anxiety. Choose one or two of the following prompts and write about something that is bringing you gratitude.

— Gratitude Journal Writing Prompts —

☐ Sit quietly and take a deep breath. When you think of the word "gratitude," what is the first thing that comes to your mind?

☐ What is one thing you love about yourself that no one else notices? Something that makes you say, "I'm glad to be me!"

☐ What is one hard thing that happened in your past that you have overcome? How does it make you feel to know you overcame a struggle?

☐ What is something special, unique, or extraordinary about yourself?

☐ What is one thing that made you smile this week? Write about it in detail.

☐ When was the last time you cracked up? What made you laugh so hard?

☐ Write about the best day you have ever had in your life.

☐ How can you do more random acts of kindness each day?

☐ If you could only use one positive word to describe today, what would it be? Why?

☐ What is something that you really appreciate because it makes your life easier?

☐ What is something you've done this week to make you feel good about yourself?

☐ What is your favorite piece of art or music? How does it make you feel?

☐ What sounds bring you peace? Explain why.

☐ Where is your favorite place in the world? Describe it and explain how it makes you feel, using all your senses.

☐ Where in the world do you feel the safest?

☐ What is the best thing that has happened today? What did you appreciate about it?

☐ When was the last time you told someone, "Thank you"? What made you thank them?

☐ How did you turn a negative moment or time into a positive one?

☐ What is a family tradition that you value? Why?

☐ How has your favorite movie or book impacted your life?

☐ What is a positive trait of a friend? How does that make them special?

☐ Who is one person you know who seems to always express their gratitude? What can you learn about them?

☐ Who is someone you can always count on to be there for you when you need them? Write about how they have supported you in the past.

☐ Who is your favorite musical artist? Why do you love their music?

☐ Who is your hero and why?

☐ Who is someone who has inspired you in the last week? How?

☐ Who is one person in your life who loves you unconditionally? How does this person make you feel? How do you know they love you unconditionally?

☐ Who is an under-appreciated worker we should be thankful for? Why?

☐ In what ways does your pet make you smile?

☐ Who has made you smile today? How can you make someone else smile?

☐ What is your favorite type of weather? Why do you enjoy days like this?

☐ What is one thing that you love about the sun? Dirt? Grass?

☐ What did the weather look like on your very best or favorite day?

☐ What is one thing about the night that makes it special?

☐ Wherever you are right now, look around and find three things you are thankful that exist. Explain why you are grateful for these things.

15-MINUTE FOCUS
Anxiety Workbook: Tips and Strategies to Manage Anxiety, Build Resilience, and Foster Emotional Well-Being

133

Gratitude Journal

134

15-MINUTE FOCUS
Anxiety Workbook: Tips and Strategies to Manage Anxiety, Build Resilience, and Foster Emotional Well-Being

Can vs. Should

Believing you **can** do something comes from a place of curiosity and confidence.
Believing you **should** do something comes from a place of judgment.
Learn to approach yourself with "can" instead of "should."

——— CAN ———

What is something you feel like you **can** do?

_____

_____

_____

_____

Why do you feel like you **can** do it?

_____

_____

_____

_____

Do you **want** to do it?

_____

_____

_____

_____

——— SHOULD ———

What is something you feel like you **should** do?

_____

_____

_____

_____

Why do you feel you **should** do it?

_____

_____

_____

_____

Do you **want** to do it?

_____

_____

_____

_____

Be **curious** not **judgmental**.

15-MINUTE FOCUS
Anxiety Workbook: Tips and Strategies to Manage Anxiety, Build Resilience, and Foster Emotional Well-Being

135

Social Media

Social anxiety can be quickly exacerbated by negative messaging and posts on social media.

Creating a student-led campaign to promote positive social media usage among middle or high school students serves to enhance digital literacy skills in addition to furthering awareness of the impact social media can have on students. There are many platforms and directions a social media campaign can take. It is important to encourage student voices in the development and implementation process, so the campaign becomes more relatable and impactful. The aim is to empower students to take ownership of their online experiences and to foster a culture of kindness, empathy, and support on social media platforms.

It is also important that the project follows district guidelines for social media activity. Consider engaging your district communications department for support.

Social Media Campaign Examples

(Middle, High)

Social Media Awareness Workshop

Organize a workshop led by a student committee to raise awareness about the impact of negative social media usage. Use examples and scenarios to highlight the consequences of cyberbullying and hurtful behavior.

Positive Social Media Guidelines

Have students collaborate to create a set of positive social media guidelines. These guidelines should emphasize empathy, respect, and the importance of standing up against cyberbullying. This could be in collaboration with an English or Social Studies/History teacher.

Artistic Expression

Engage students in creating posters, artwork, and infographics that convey positive messages about social media usage. These can be displayed throughout the school to reinforce the campaign's goals.

Video Campaign

Encourage students to create short videos that showcase positive ways to use social media. These videos can include skits, interviews, or testimonials from students sharing their experiences with online kindness.

Social Media Pledge

Design a pledge for students to commit to using social media in a positive manner. Have a signing event where students publicly pledge their support for the campaign.

Peer-to-Peer Workshops

Train a group of students to conduct interactive workshops in classrooms. These workshops can cover topics like building a positive online community, recognizing and stopping cyberbullying, and promoting mental health awareness. This could also be done in collaboration with a content-area teacher as project-based learning.

15-MINUTE FOCUS
Anxiety Workbook: Tips and Strategies to Manage Anxiety, Build Resilience, and Foster Emotional Well-Being

137

Guest Speaker Series

Invite local influencers, educators, or mental health professionals to give talks on the importance of responsible social media usage and its impact on mental health.

Kindness Challenges

Launch weekly or monthly kindness challenges that students can participate in and share on social media. For example, challenge them to compliment a friend publicly, share a positive quote, or showcase acts of kindness they witness.

Social Media Scavenger Hunt

Organize a scavenger hunt that requires students to find positive and uplifting content on social media platforms. This activity encourages students to actively seek out good examples online.

Peer Support Networks

Establish peer support networks or groups where students can share their concerns about social media and discuss ways to help and support each other. These groups should be facilitated with the school counselor, school social worker, or other school-based mental health provider.

Caregiver Involvement and Awareness

Host an event where students provide caregivers with resources to support their children in navigating social media positively.

Social Media and Digital Literacy

(Elementary, Middle, High)

The established connection between social anxiety and social media creates an opportunity to provide students with education and training on positive social media habits and digital literacy. There is a wealth of resources available to support this effort.

Common Sense's free **Digital Citizenship Curriculum** addresses critical issues facing children in a fast-changing world of media and technology. The innovative lessons teach students to think critically and develop the habits of mind to navigate digital dilemmas in their everyday lives. It was created in collaboration with Project Zero at the Harvard Graduate School of Education, guided by research with thousands of educators and caregivers. The **Digital Citizenship Curriculum** includes 73 lessons across 13 grades (for ages 5 to 18), with 32 videos. https://www.commonsense.org/education/digital-citizenship/curriculum

Also from Common Sense and Cornell University, **Social Media Test Drive** is a free web-based educational program that offers twelve impressive modules about key digital citizenship topics, such as managing privacy settings, self-presentation and identity online, responding to or preventing cyberbullying, and analyzing news and information students could encounter through social media. More information can be found at https://www.commonsense.org/education/social-media-test-drive.

Caregiver Information on Social Anxiety and Social Media

Below you will find two versions of information you can provide to caregivers regarding Social Anxiety. One includes tips about social media and the other does not, depending on the age level or needs of the child.

Understanding and Supporting Your Child's Social Anxiety

As our children navigate their way through different stages of their education, they may encounter various challenges, including social anxiety. Social anxiety is a common psychological condition that affects children of all ages, from elementary school to high school. As caregivers, it's crucial to recognize this issue and provide the necessary support for our children so they can thrive both academically and emotionally.

What is Social Anxiety?

Social anxiety is an overwhelming fear of social situations or interactions that involve the possibility of being judged or evaluated. It can manifest differently depending on the age of the child and the specific context. While it is natural to feel nervous in social situations, social anxiety becomes problematic when it significantly hinders a child's ability to engage with others, make friends, or participate in activities they would otherwise enjoy.

Symptoms of Social Anxiety

- **Physical manifestations:** Children of all ages may experience physical symptoms such as sweating, trembling, stomachaches, headaches, or a rapid heartbeat when faced with social situations.
- **Avoidance:** Children might actively avoid social gatherings, group activities, or even simple conversations with peers, teachers, or other adults.
- **Fear of judgment:** Students with social anxiety often fear being judged or embarrassed in social settings, leading to a reluctance to speak up or participate in class discussions.
- **Overthinking and self-criticism:** Children might excessively worry about how others perceive them, leading to negative self-talk and feelings of inadequacy.

Strategies to Support Your Child

- **Create a safe and supportive environment:** Foster an atmosphere of open communication and understanding at home. Reassure your child that it is okay to feel nervous in social situations and that you are there to help and support them.
- **Gradual exposure:** Encourage your child to face their fears gradually. Start with small social interactions and build up to more challenging situations at a pace that feels comfortable for them.

15-MINUTE FOCUS
Anxiety Workbook: Tips and Strategies to Manage Anxiety, Build Resilience, and Foster Emotional Well-Being

139

- **Teach coping skills:** Help your child learn relaxation techniques, such as deep breathing or mindfulness, to manage anxiety when it arises.
- **Model appropriate social skills:** Demonstrate and practice social interactions with your child, offering guidance and feedback on appropriate behavior in different situations.
- **Seek professional help:** If your child's social anxiety significantly impacts their daily life, consider seeking support from a mental health professional who specializes in treating anxiety in children.

Discussion Starters for Conversations with Children

Many children are afraid to talk about their feelings of anxiety. Having a trusted adult initiate the conversation can actually reduce their anxiety. The most effective discussions take place when the child is feeling calm and secure in a comfortable environment. Here are some questions that can help you start conversations with your child about the anxiety they experience:

- "Sometimes, meeting new people can be scary. Is there anything that makes you feel nervous when talking to new friends or adults?"
- "I remember feeling a bit nervous when I was your age too. What do you think we can do together to make those situations easier for you?"
- "It's natural to feel a little shy or anxious sometimes. Would you like to share a story about a time when you felt really confident in a social setting?"
- "If you ever feel overwhelmed, remember that we're here to listen and help. What can we do to support you when you're feeling anxious?"
- "Everyone has different strengths, and it's okay to be yourself. What are some things that make you unique and special?"

By understanding social anxiety and providing appropriate support, caregivers can help their children develop coping skills and navigate social situations with greater confidence. Remember that every child is unique, and a little understanding and compassion can go a long way in helping them overcome their social anxiety and thrive in their social interactions. If you or your child need additional assistance, please reach out to the school counselor for support. We are here to partner with you for your student's success.

Helping Your Child Navigate Social Anxiety and Social Media

Social anxiety is a common challenge that many students face as they progress through their academic years. From elementary school through high school, children may experience overwhelming fear and nervousness in social situations. Social media plays a significant role in the increase of students reporting symptoms associated with social anxiety. Social media can affect children's well-being and anxiety levels. Social media platforms can create feelings of comparison, insecurity, and pressure to maintain a certain image, which may exacerbate anxiety in some individuals. Although social media can be entertaining and educational, it can also be used as a platform to bully, harass, isolate, and judge others, putting students who experience social anxiety at greater risk. As caregivers, understanding social anxiety, its symptoms, and providing support is crucial to help your child build confidence and thrive in their social interactions.

What is Social Anxiety?

Social anxiety is an overwhelming fear of social situations or interactions that involve the possibility of being judged or evaluated. It goes beyond the typical shyness and can significantly impact a child's ability to make friends, engage in group activities, or participate in class discussions.

Symptoms of Social Anxiety

- **Physical signs:** Children may exhibit physical symptoms such as blushing, sweating, trembling, or a rapid heartbeat when faced with social situations.
- **Avoidance:** Kids might actively avoid social events or gatherings, preferring to be alone rather than risk feeling uncomfortable in social settings.
- **Fear of judgment:** Students with social anxiety often worry excessively about being judged or embarrassed in front of others, leading to a reluctance to speak up or share their thoughts.
- **Negative self-perception:** Children may have a negative self-image and perceive themselves as inadequate or unlikable.
- **Social Media:** Students who experience social anxiety as a result of activity on social media may spend more time engaging on social media apps, searching for posts and comments about themselves often reinforcing their feelings of anxiety.

Strategies to Support Your Child

- **Foster a safe and supportive environment:** Create an open and non-judgmental atmosphere at home where your child feels comfortable discussing their feelings and fears.
- **Encourage small steps:** Encourage your child to face their fears gradually. Start with low-pressure social situations and celebrate their achievements, no matter how small.
- **Set healthy boundaries:** Establish guidelines for social media usage, such as limiting screen time and encouraging device-free moments.
- **Encourage off-line activities:** Encourage your child to participate in hobbies, sports, and spend quality time with friends and family in person.
- **Discuss online safety:** Teach your child about online safety, privacy, and the importance of reporting any harmful or concerning content.
- **Be an active participant:** Engage with your child on social media platforms to better understand their online experiences and provide guidance when needed.
- **Teach coping techniques:** Help your child develop coping skills, such as deep breathing, positive affirmations, or visualization, to manage anxiety when it arises.
- **Seek professional help if needed:** If social anxiety significantly impacts your child's daily life, consider consulting a mental health professional who specializes in anxiety in children.

Discussion Starters for Conversations with Children

Many children are afraid to talk about their feelings of anxiety. Having a trusted adult initiate the conversation can actually reduce their anxiety. The most effective discussions take place when the child

15-MINUTE FOCUS
Anxiety Workbook: Tips and Strategies to Manage Anxiety, Build Resilience, and Foster Emotional Well-Being

141

is feeling calm and secure in a comfortable environment. Here are some questions that can help you start conversations with your child about their anxiety:

- "I noticed you might sometimes feel uneasy in social situations. Can you tell me more about how you feel, so I can understand better and support you?"

- "Socializing can be challenging sometimes, but it's okay to take things one step at a time. What do you think we can do together to make social situations more comfortable for you?"

- "How important is social media to you and your peers? What kind of posts do you see regularly on social media?"

- "Has anyone ever mentioned you in their social media posts? What kinds of things were said about you? How did that make you feel?"

- "If you ever feel anxious in a social situation, I want you to know that you can always talk to me about it. How can I help you feel more at ease?"

Social Media Resources for Caregivers

- Common Sense Media (www.commonsensemedia.org) provides reviews and age-appropriate recommendations for movies, TV shows, books, games, and apps.

- The American Academy of Pediatrics Parenting website (www.healthychildren.org) offers guidelines on screen time for children and adolescents as well as mental health resources.

- Child Mind Institute (www.childmind.org) provides resources and articles on various mental health topics, including anxiety and social media usage.

By supporting your child in navigating social anxiety and managing social media usage mindfully, you can help them develop healthy coping mechanisms and foster positive relationships both in person and online. Remember that open communication and understanding play a vital role in nurturing your child's emotional well-being. If you or your child need additional assistance, please reach out to the school counselor for support. We are here to partner with you for your student's success.

142

15-MINUTE FOCUS
Anxiety Workbook: Tips and Strategies to Manage Anxiety, Build Resilience, and Foster Emotional Well-Being

Let's Check-in with Our Students

How did the school staff at our students' school support them?

Amelia

Amelia's parents contacted the school counselor with their concerns. The school counselor facilitated a student support meeting with Amelia's parents and her teacher. Amelia was even able to attend after the adults discussed strategies to address the situation. The school counselor is providing small group counseling with Amelia and three other students who experience similar symptoms to practice social and interpersonal skills in a structured environment, with the goal of increasing the students' self-confidence in social interactions. Amelia's teachers are providing extra encouragement and giving her opportunities to contribute in ways that feel comfortable to her. Finally, Amelia's parents scheduled an appointment with their pediatrician to rule out any medical causes and discussed a referral for a psychologist for family counseling.

Amelia has begun to show improvement. She is reporting less anxious feelings and is starting to form healthy friendships. Her teacher reports an increase in participation in class as well as improved academic performance. It has been a challenging journey, but the support her school and family have offered Amelia have created a positive and nurturing environment to overcome her social anxiety and flourish.

Jaime

After receiving a newsletter about cyberbullying, Jaime's parents recognize some of the symptoms that they have been exhibiting. They decide to have an open conversation with Jaime about their recent behavior and struggles. Together, they all decide to practice healthy social media habits and exchange time spent on devices with more family time together.

After the family conversation, Jaime meets with their school counselor to seek support in dealing with their anxiety. The school counselor works with Jaime to develop coping strategies for managing social anxiety, specifically using Cognitive Behavioral Therapy to help Jaime challenge negative thought patterns, set realistic expectations, and build social skills. The counselor also collaborates with the school to promote a culture of empathy and inclusivity, reducing instances of online bullying and peer pressure.

Gradually, with the support of their parents, school counselor, and teachers, Jaime begins to develop healthier habits regarding social media use. They learn to navigate online interactions with more resilience and to differentiate between meaningful connections and superficial validation. Their self-esteem improves, and they feel more confident in expressing themselves both online and off-line. As a result, they experience improvements in their academic performance, emotional well-being, social relationships, and overall physical health.

15-MINUTE FOCUS
Anxiety Workbook: Tips and Strategies to Manage Anxiety, Build Resilience, and Foster Emotional Well-Being

143

Samira

As a result of a lesson with the school counselor about social anxiety, Samira believes she now has a name for what she has been experiencing. She begins meeting with the school counselor regularly to explore her feelings and thoughts about her cultural identity and how to discuss these feelings with her parents. Samira also learns coping strategies, such as deep breathing exercises and mindfulness techniques, to manage her anxiety in social situations. The school counselor also works with her to build social skills and self-confidence, encouraging her to express her unique perspective and cultural identity proudly. With her permission, teachers are also made aware of Samira's social anxiety and are encouraged to provide additional support and understanding during classroom interactions.

Samira is becoming more comfortable expressing herself and participating in social activities. Her academic performance improves as she gains confidence in her abilities, and she starts forming meaningful friendships based on mutual understanding and respect. Most notably, Samira was able to open up to her parents about her concerns. She was pleasantly surprised to find they were more open to discuss how she can fully explore her newer American experiences while also embracing her cultural identity.

144

15-MINUTE FOCUS
Anxiety Workbook: Tips and Strategies to Manage Anxiety, Build Resilience, and Foster Emotional Well-Being

CHAPTER FIVE

Performance Anxiety

What is Performance Anxiety?

Performance anxiety is a type of anxiety that typically develops in anticipation of or during presentations, performances, or competitive situations. It can affect students of all ages, particularly in areas such as public speaking, visual and performing arts, sports, and competitions. Performance anxiety differs from general anxiety because it involves specific situations where a student is required to perform or present in front of others. It often involves worries about being scrutinized or making mistakes during the performance.

Symptoms of Performance Anxiety

Symptoms of performance anxiety can range in intensity from mild to severe, present differently based on the type of performance, and may vary from one student to another.

Mild Symptoms

- Slight nervousness or jitters before a performance.
- Minor physical symptoms such as a slightly elevated heart rate or butterflies in the stomach.
- Mild self-doubt and worry about the upcoming performance.

Moderate Symptoms

- Increased anxiety and restlessness leading up to the performance.
- Physical symptoms such as sweaty palms, trembling, or dry mouth.
- Difficulty focusing and organizing thoughts due to heightened stress.

Severe Symptoms

- Intense fear and panic before and during the performance.
- Significant physical symptoms such as nausea, rapid heartbeat, shortness of breath, and panic attacks.
- Impaired cognitive functioning, including memory loss and confusion.
- Strong desire to avoid the performance altogether.

15-MINUTE FOCUS
Anxiety Workbook: Tips and Strategies to Manage Anxiety, Build Resilience, and Foster Emotional Well-Being

145

Impact of Performance Anxiety on Students

Performance anxiety can affect students in various ways.

Academically

- Lowered academic performance in activities that involve public speaking, presentations, or performances.
- Difficulty expressing knowledge and skills during the performance due to anxiety-related impairments.

Emotionally

- Intense fear, worry, and self-consciousness.
- Negative impact on self-esteem and self-confidence.
- Increased stress and emotional distress.

Physically

- Physical symptoms such as headaches, stomachaches, muscle tension, and fatigue.
- Impact on overall health and well-being due to chronic stress.

Socially

- Avoidance of social situations that involve performance or competition.
- Strained relationships with peers due to avoidance behaviors.
- Difficulty forming new relationships or participating in group activities.

Student Stories

Taos

Taos is a 9-year-old Hispanic student attending Hawthorne Elementary School. He is an energetic and creative young boy often writing and illustrating stories about his favorite movie characters. However, anytime Taos' teacher asks him to share his tales with the class, he shuts down and his bright eyes become clouded with anxiety and worry. Mrs. Todd has noticed similar reactions during group activities. Taos' face flushes, voice quivers, and he often stumbles over words. Taos also becomes distressed when the teacher calls his name to participate in discussions, and he frequently comes up with excuses for not completing assignments that include any type of oral presentation. His performance anxiety makes it challenging for him to express his knowledge effectively.

At home, Taos' family has noticed several signs of his performance anxiety. When they encourage him to share his artwork or read stories he has written, Taos becomes visibly nervous and hesitant. His hands tremble and he tends to avoid eye contact. Despite their efforts to create a supportive environment, Taos feels overwhelmed and fearful of disappointing his family, leading him to have a negative self-concept. These self-perceptions, coupled with fears of being judged by his peers, are keeping Taos from engaging in social interactions and building meaningful connections with others.

Micah

Middle school has been challenging for Micah, a 13-year-old African American female attending Maplewood Middle School for the Arts. She is extremely gifted in music, particularly in playing the guitar and singing. Micah has recorded and released multiple songs over social media and has developed quite a following. The choir director, Mrs. Kassidy, has spoken to Micah multiple times about joining the performance choir; however, she politely declines the invitations for one reason. Micah suffers from performance anxiety.

Despite her incredible talent and viral approval, the thought of performing in front of a live audience causes Micah significant bouts of anxiety. In previous attempts to play her music for small groups of friends, Micah experienced racing heartbeats, sweating, dry mouth, and a shaky voice, all of which made it very difficult for her to sing. Her hands trembled, which interrupted her ability to play the guitar. When she is able to move beyond the physical symptoms, Micah often forgets the words to her songs. She feels embarrassed and humiliated. Micah is worried the other students at the school of the arts will not understand her anxiety, so she keeps everyone at a distance. She believes the only way to use and share her talent is to make music by herself and release recordings online, as she has been doing, or let someone else perform it.

Micah shares her musical talent with several members of her family. During impromptu family musical sessions, Micah's parents have noticed an increase in symptoms related to performance anxiety. She starts fidgeting, avoids eye contact, and finds reasons to excuse herself from the group. Micah's parents enrolled her in the arts school to help foster and develop her musical talents, but they are growing more concerned that her performance anxiety will hinder Micah's opportunity to advance her skills.

15-MINUTE FOCUS
Anxiety Workbook: Tips and Strategies to Manage Anxiety, Build Resilience, and Foster Emotional Well-Being

147

Kessler

Kessler is a 17-year-old senior attending Crescent High School in his suburban community. Kessler grew up playing soccer, first for recreation leagues, and then advancing to competitive teams. When he enrolled at Crescent High School, the soccer coach was pleased when Kessler attended the team try outs. His skills won him a spot on the varsity team and Kessler became a valuable member of the team. Over the years, they won district, regional, and even a state championship. Recently, the accolades brought additional attention to Kessler and his skills on the soccer field. Recruiters from university soccer teams as well as some professional leagues began attending his games and contacting his family. Coach Browne talked to Kessler about the likelihood of receiving athletic scholarships to attend college. Kessler found the extra attention a bit uncomfortable. He began to struggle on the field, missing shots that once were automatic. When his teammates offered encouragement, Kessler responded with angry retorts. He experienced more physical issues such as muscle tension, increased fatigue, and heart palpitations. Kessler's growing frustration with his performance on the soccer field spilled over into the classroom. He had trouble concentrating in class, completing assignments, and when a teacher called on him to answer questions, Kessler's mind would go blank and he would not be able to offer a reasonable, let alone correct, answer.

At home, Kessler spent more time outside practicing his skills. His parents grew concerned that the changes in his behaviors, demeanor, and performance were more than just a slump. They noticed that any time a recruiter came to visit, Kessler would grow quiet and find reasons to excuse himself from the conversations. When they tried to talk to him about their concerns, Kessler would shut down and say he was tired.

Manage Performance Anxiety by Redefining Success

ELEMENTARY, MIDDLE, HIGH

LESSON LENGTH	25-40 minutes
OBJECTIVES	• Students will define performance anxiety. • Students will construct healthy definitions of success as a strategy to manage and reduce performance anxiety.
MATERIALS	• Success Means Worksheet (Elementary only) • Colored pencils, markers, or crayons (Elementary only)

2-5 MINUTES · Introduction

- Welcome students and introduce objectives of the lesson.
- If other lessons on anxiety have been taught previously, ask students to recall prior knowledge so they can connect it to new knowledge about performance anxiety.

7-10 MINUTES · What is Performance Anxiety?

- Explain what performance anxiety is.

  Performance Anxiety *is a type of anxiety that typically develops in anticipation of or during presentations, performances, or competitive situations. It can affect students of all ages, particularly in areas such as public speaking, visual and performing arts, sports, and competitions. It often involves worries about being evaluated or making mistakes during the performance.*

- Ask students to share what types of situations might cause someone to get anxious. Provide prompts appropriate for the age group:

  - **Elementary School Students:** asking questions in class, reading aloud in class, performing or playing a musical instrument on stage, playing on a sports team.

15-MINUTE FOCUS
Anxiety Workbook: Tips and Strategies to Manage Anxiety, Build Resilience, and Foster Emotional Well-Being

149

- **Middle School Students:** in addition to previous situations, doing an oral presentation, participating in a group project, giving a speech, being in a play.

- **High School Students:** in addition to previous situations, interviewing for a job, some work situations, interviewing for postsecondary applications, leadership positions, participating in project-based learning presentations.

- Describe the symptoms of performance anxiety. Point out that symptoms can vary by student and by performance type.

  Mild Symptoms include slight nervousness or jitters before a performance, slightly elevated heart rate or butterflies in the stomach, and mild self-doubt and worry about an upcoming performance.

  Moderate Symptoms include increased anxiety and restlessness leading up to the performance, sweaty palms, trembling, or dry mouth, and difficulty focusing and organizing thoughts due to heightened stress.

  Severe Symptoms include intense fear and panic before and during the performance, nausea, rapid heartbeat, shortness of breath, panic attacks, memory loss and confusion about the content of the performance, and a strong desire to avoid the performance altogether.

- Have students imagine what it would be like trying to complete a presentation or performance if experiencing those symptoms. If you have a confident student who would like to role play, invite them to the front of the room and instruct them to act as if they are experiencing several of the symptoms of performance anxiety. Next ask them to recite a short poem, the ABCs, sing a verse of a song, etc. Then allow them to share the challenges they felt.

- Remind students:

  Anxiety is not a choice but a reaction to a real or perceived threat or fear. We are going to explore the fear or threat that drives performance anxiety.

Defining Success

3 MINUTES

- Explain that much like test anxiety, the fear of failure is at the root of performance anxiety.

  *Prior to and during a performance, **fear about not meeting expectations** creeps in and takes hold, causing our amygdala to sense a threat to our safety. Depending on the type of performance, the threat is typically our emotional or social safety. However, we may fear that mistakes during our performance can impact future opportunities as in scholarships, awards, etc. Sometimes, in athletic competitions the anxiety can cause us to perform in such a way that we risk physical injury.*

- One strategy that helps to lessen our fear of failure and reduce our performance anxiety is to assess how we define success and failure.

150

15-MINUTE FOCUS
Anxiety Workbook: Tips and Strategies to Manage Anxiety, Build Resilience, and Foster Emotional Well-Being

10
MINUTES

How Do You Define Success? (Elementary)

- Lead a conversation about the definition of success and failure. Younger students may need a concrete example to help conceptualize the ideas of success and failure.

  What does success mean on a spelling test? Is a perfect score of 100 a success? Is it possible to miss some words and still be successful?

- Repeat with failure.

  What does failure mean on a spelling test? If failure when you get a particular failing grade? What if a student missed nine out of ten spelling words on the practice test earlier in the week, and on the final test, the student missed six out of ten words. Is that still failure? Does anyone think that could be success?

- Help students understand that success and failure can have different meanings.

  If we are preparing for a performance and feeling anxiety, we can control the anxiety by determining what we think it means to be successful and what it means to fail.

- Distribute the **Success Means Worksheet** and **colored pencils, markers, or crayons**. While students color the worksheet, discuss the examples of success:

  - **Doing My Best:** When we try hard and give our best effort, we can be proud regardless of the outcome.

  - **Making Improvements:** Recognizing growth in our performance area is important to our success. We often do not start at the very top of the talent pool. We have to practice to improve our skills.

  - **Celebrating My Effort:** It is important to work toward goals. It is also important to acknowledge the hard work that we put into achieving our goals, even before we meet them.

  - **Only Comparing Myself to Myself:** It is easy to compare ourselves to other people and decide that we are not good enough.

  - **Being Brave:** Performing in front of others requires courage. Honor taking the step even though you may feel nervous or afraid.

  - There is an empty circle if students want to add their own definition of what success means to them.

15-MINUTE FOCUS
Anxiety Workbook: Tips and Strategies to Manage Anxiety, Build Resilience, and Foster Emotional Well-Being

151

How Do You Define Success? (Middle, High)

- Divide the class into small groups. Have them discuss the definitions of success and failure. After several minutes ask each group to share a summary of their conversation with the class. Highlight any differences noted in the definitions the students discussed.

   If we understand that success and failure can have different meanings when we are preparing for a performance and feeling anxiety, we can control the anxiety by determining what we think it means to be successful and what it means to fail, and then redefining those.

- Share video clip from the movie *Sing, Meena,* in which the main character overcomes performance anxiety to sing *Don't You Worry 'Bout a Thing* (https://www.youtube.com/watch?v=bfTv6A1Wn4k)

   Meena had previously failed when she tried to audition and lacked confidence to perform even though she wanted to perform.

- Have students identify her initial definition of success and failure.

   Because she made mistakes at the audition, she did not believe she was going to achieve her goal of performing on stage. What happened when Mr. Moon helped Meena see that success means "just sing"?

- An important part of this discussion for our middle and high school students is the recognition that sometimes there are definitions of success that cannot be changed. For example, grades in schools, scores on tests, points on a scoreboard, etc. This is an opportunity to discuss the idea that these measures are only one way to define success. There are standard measures for some activities that we participate in that will determine success based on achievement. When we focus on **achievement measures of success**, that often increases anxiety. However, if we shift the focus from **achievement to effort**, that reduces anxiety.

- Review the examples of success generated by students. For those examples that focus on achievement, ask students to consider ways to revise it so that it focuses on effort. For example:

   RECITE the assigned poem without any errors revised to PRACTICE the assigned poem and deliver it with feeling.

- Allow students to explore how revising those definitions changes how they feel about the proposed performance.

   Adopting definitions of success based on effort rather than achievement and perfection sets us up for approaching performances with confidence in ourselves, which reduces the fear that fuels performance anxiety.

152

15-MINUTE FOCUS
Anxiety Workbook: Tips and Strategies to Manage Anxiety, Build Resilience, and Foster Emotional Well-Being

Wrap Up & Assessment

- **Elementary School Students:**

    - Encourage students to color their worksheet and keep it as a reminder that success can mean a lot more than winning or getting a perfect score.

    - Remind students that if they experience performance anxiety they can reach out to a teacher, coach, or the school counselor for support.

- **Middle and High School Students:**

    - Encourage students to remember that success can mean a lot more than winning or getting a perfect score.

    - Remind students that if they experience performance anxiety they can reach out to a teacher, coach, or the school counselor for support.

15-MINUTE FOCUS
Anxiety Workbook: Tips and Strategies to Manage Anxiety, Build Resilience, and Foster Emotional Well-Being

153

NAME: _____

ONLY COMPARING MYSELF TO MYSELF

BEING BRAVE

SUCCESS MEANS

Write or draw what success means to you.

CELEBRATING MY EFFORT

DOING MY BEST

MAKING IMPROVEMENTS

Classroom Accommodations

Classroom accommodations for students with performance anxiety can help create a supportive and understanding environment that allows students to thrive academically and emotionally. Remember that each student is unique, and the accommodations should be tailored to their specific needs. Engage the student, caregiver, school counselor and/or school social worker to identify helpful accommodations.

- **Flexible Presentation Options:** Allow students to choose from various presentation formats, such as written reports, visual displays, or multimedia projects, to accommodate different learning styles and reduce the pressure of public speaking.
- **Small Group or Individual Presentations:** Offer opportunities for students to present in smaller groups or one-on-one with the teacher to help them feel more comfortable and less overwhelmed.
- **Preparation and Practice:** Provide ample time for students to practice their presentations or performances in a safe and supportive setting. This can help build their confidence and reduce anxiety.
- **Positive Reinforcement:** Recognize and praise students' efforts and progress, rather than solely focusing on their performance outcomes. Positive feedback can boost their self-esteem and motivation.
- **Cue Cards or Notes:** Allow students to use cue cards or brief notes during presentations to help them remember key points and reduce anxiety about forgetting information.
- **Encourage Self-Advocacy:** Teach students to advocate for themselves and communicate their needs to teachers, allowing for a more supportive and understanding approach.
- **Audio/Video Recording:** Allow students to record their presentations or performances if they find it helpful for self-assessment or to share with the teacher privately.

Individual Counseling Interventions for Students Experiencing Performance Anxiety

The following worksheets can be used with individual students to help them learn about performance anxiety, understand their own experience with performance anxiety, identify strategies to better manage their performance anxiety, and practice coping skills to reduce their performance anxiety. Instructions and probing questions to help students process the content of the activities are suggested below.

Defining Success

Performance anxiety is fueled by a fear of failing during a performance or presentation. Students experiencing performance anxiety often adopt unrealistic expectations regarding their performance. They fear that any mistake will shatter all chances of success. Their effort will be a failure. Cognitive Behavioral Therapy is an effective approach to challenge faulty thinking and cognitive distortions that feed students' performance anxiety. Here are a series of activities that help students better manage their anxiety before presentations and performances by redefining success.

15-MINUTE FOCUS
Anxiety Workbook: Tips and Strategies to Manage Anxiety, Build Resilience, and Foster Emotional Well-Being

155

(Elementary)

Hand out the **How Do You Define Success? Worksheet (Elementary).** Help the student think through various ways that they can be successful (completing a project, winning a game, etc.). If they offer examples that suggest scoring a perfect score or grade, acknowledge that although those are measures of success, they often can add to our anxiety because they shift our focus to achievement. When we prioritize effort and doing our best, we can lessen the anxiety we feel. As the student demonstrates an understanding of expanding the definition of success, ask them to redefine what success means for the performance or presentation that is causing them anxiety in the top box. Then have them imagine how it would feel to achieve that success. Encourage the student to approach their performance with their new definition of success.

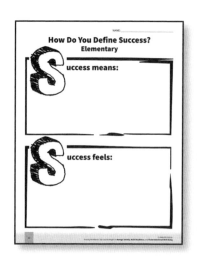

(Middle)

Hand out the **How Do You Define Success? Worksheet (Middle).** Help the student think through various ways that they can be successful (completing a project, winning a game, etc.). If they offer examples that suggest scoring a perfect score or grade, acknowledge that although those are measures of success, they often can add to our anxiety because they shift our focus to achievement. When we prioritize effort and doing our best, we can lessen the anxiety we feel. Assist the student in redefining success to focus on effort rather than a specific achievement. Once they have a definition of success, work with them to identify what success will look like in specific areas of their life: home, school, and with friends.

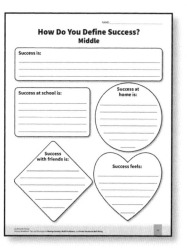

Next, ask the student to imagine how achieving their new definition of success will feel to them. Finally, ask them to apply this process of revising what success means to their performance or presentation.

(High)

Pass out the **How Do you Define Success? Worksheet (High)**. Ask the student to define success. If they offer examples that suggest scoring a perfect score or grade, acknowledge that although those are measures of success, they often can add to our anxiety because they shift our focus to achievement. When we prioritize effort and doing our best, we can lessen the anxiety we feel. Assist the student in redefining success to focus on effort rather than a specific achievement. Once they have a definition of success, help them to identify what they can do to meet their new expectation of success.

Next, have the student brainstorm how they will know when they have achieved success. Finally, encourage the student to imagine what it will feel like to achieve success. When they have mastered the process of revising their meaning of success and recognizing success, assist them in applying the process to their performance or presentation.

Success Breeds Success

(Older Elementary, Middle, High)

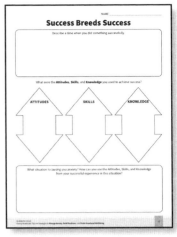

Research has shown that when we achieve success, we can build on that success and often earn more success. We have more confidence and self-efficacy. This intervention is based on those principles.

Pass out the **Success Breeds Success Worksheet**. Ask the student to recall a time when they achieved success. Let them describe the situation, paying attention to what they believed, what they did, and what they learned in order to realize success. The student can summarize their successful experience in the first box. Next, help the student identify the attitudes, skills, and knowledge that they used to achieve success. They can list those in the respective arrows. Finally, ask the student to identify a specific situation that is causing them anxiety. Work with the student to identify how they can use the attitude, skills, and knowledge from the previous situation to achieve success in this one.

Asset Building

Recognizing their inherent and unique value can serve to protect students from negative thoughts that contribute to the fear of failure that drives performance anxiety. Helping a child identify their unique qualities, talents, or skills will help them see how they can contribute and make their environment better.

(Elementary)

Distribute the **Asset Building Worksheet (Elementary).** As the student is writing what makes them special in the building blocks, help them see how they use those special traits to show kindness, respect, trustworthiness, responsibility, citizenship, compassion, creativity, problem-solving skills, hope, self-control, etc. When possible, highlight connections between the student's special traits and their performance or presentation concerns. Assist the student in identifying talents, skills, attitudes, perspectives, and attributes they embody that they can share with their family, school, community, and world. Some students may need help conceptualizing their community and world. The focus should be on their individuality and unique gifts as positive and valuable.

(Middle, High)

Pass out the **Asset Building Worksheet (Middle/High).** Ask the student to identify one of their most valued strengths and write it on the award ribbon. Next have the student recognize how they use their strength to help their family, friends, school, community, and world in each of the respective blocks. As they are identifying how they contribute in positive ways, ask them what it feels like knowing that they are able to support so many people. If possible, highlight any connection between the student's strength and the performance or presentation that is causing them anxiety. Reinforce that even though the student makes mistakes, they are still able to contribute in positive ways.

15-MINUTE FOCUS
Anxiety Workbook: Tips and Strategies to Manage Anxiety, Build Resilience, and Foster Emotional Well-Being

157

How Do You Define Success?
Elementary

uccess means:

uccess feels:

How Do You Define Success?
Middle

Success is:

_____

_____

_____

Success at school is:

_____

_____

_____

_____

Success at home is:

_____

_____

_____

_____

_____

Success with friends is:

_____

_____

_____

_____

Success feels:

_____

_____

_____

_____

_____

15-MINUTE FOCUS
Anxiety Workbook: Tips and Strategies to Manage Anxiety, Build Resilience, and Foster Emotional Well-Being

159

How Do You Define Success?
High

Success means...

To be successful I will...

I will know that I am successful when...

Success will feel...

160

15-MINUTE FOCUS
Anxiety Workbook: Tips and Strategies to Manage Anxiety, Build Resilience, and Foster Emotional Well-Being

Success Breeds Success

Describe a time when you did something successfully.

What were the **Attitudes**, **Skills**, and **Knowledge** you used to achieve success?

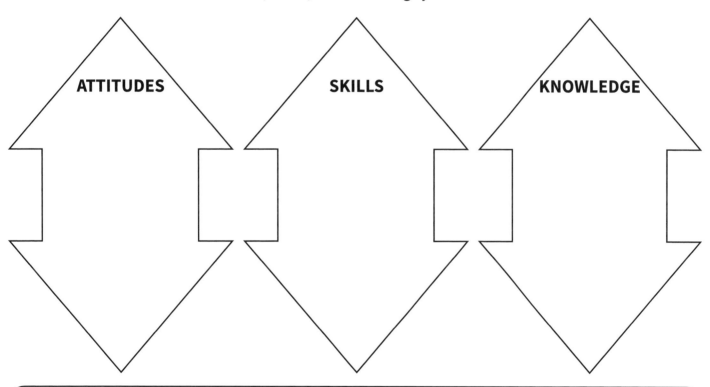

ATTITUDES   SKILLS   KNOWLEDGE

What situation is causing you anxiety? How can you use the Attitudes, Skills, and Knowledge from your successful experience in this situation?

Asset Building

3
THINGS
THAT
ONLY I
CAN OFFER

Elementary

MY WORLD

MY SCHOOL

MY COMMUNITY

MY FAMILY

_____

_____

Asset Building
Middle/High

I use my strength to help my family:

_____

_____

_____

_____

_____

I use my strength to help my friends:

_____

_____

_____

_____

_____

I use my strength to help my school:

_____

_____

_____

_____

_____

I use my strength to help my community:

_____

_____

_____

_____

_____

I use my strength to help the world:

_____

_____

_____

_____

_____

15-MINUTE FOCUS
Anxiety Workbook: Tips and Strategies to Manage Anxiety, Build Resilience, and Foster Emotional Well-Being

163

Strategies for Managing and Reducing Performance Anxiety

Students experiencing mild and some moderate performance anxiety can employ coping strategies to help manage and reduce their discomfort so they can move forward with their performance. Prevention strategies are good habits students can adopt to reduce the frequency and intensity of episodes of performance anxiety. Practicing intervention strategies before students need them will address questions about how to use them, increase comfort using them, and build confidence and agency in controlling uncomfortable feelings.

Consider teaching and practicing one or two coping strategies a week in morning meetings or advisory periods, when reviewing requirements for a presentation assignment, and again prior to students delivering their presentations, or whenever students are displaying anxious symptoms.

Prevention Strategies

Planning and Preparation

Set up a schedule to ensure students have ample time to prepare and practice for the presentation. This includes making sure they have the materials and supplies needed for the presentation.

Balancing Preparation

Students who experience performance anxiety tend to get hyper-focused on practicing for the performance. Help students identify activities they can engage in other than practice that will nurture their physical, social, and emotional selves. Suggestions include taking a 10-minute walk break, listening to your favorite song, getting a healthy snack, and talking to a friend. They return to their preparation with a fresh mind and renewed energy.

Prioritize Physical Care

It can be easy to skip meals and exchange quick naps for full nights of sleep. Eating healthy meals with produce and protein will keep the body functioning more effectively. Caffeine and sugar actually increase the frequency and intensity of anxiety symptoms. A full night's sleep of 6–8 hours allow the brain to rest, which promotes better cognitive functioning and emotional regulation.

Intervention Strategies

Deep Breathing

Inhale slowly through the nose, counting to four, and exhale slowly through the mouth, counting to eight.

Visualize Success

Students should close their eyes as they are comfortable and imagine that they have completed their performance successfully. Ask them to notice what is happening around them. How do they feel? What do they hear? What do they see? Tell them to sit with those positive feelings for a moment, then open their eyes and carry them into the performance.

Positive Self-Talk

Encourage students to replace negative thoughts with positive ones. For example, "I can do this!" instead of "I'm not good enough." Practicing exchanging positive self-talk is important as most students will find it difficult initially. This strategy can also be reinforced in academic curricula such as literature or history. When discussing a character that expresses negative self-talk, ask students to identify some positive statements the character could make instead.

Mindful Mantra

Students create a mantra, chant, or affirmation that will inspire them to focus on the joy the activity brings them, celebrate the effort they have put forth in preparation, and honor the courage they have in sharing their talent through the performance. Examples could include:

- I believe in myself.
- I can do hard things.
- It is enough to do my best.
- I prepared. I came. I slayed.
- I am using my talents and skills to bring joy into the world.

When the students feel anxiety, have them close their eyes, repeat their mantra to themselves, and pay attention to the moment. This mindful break will help them reset before beginning their performance.

Stretching

Simple stretching to release tension can help the body return to a more balanced state. Yoga stretches are great examples of stretches that students can practice to relieve their anxiety.

15-MINUTE FOCUS
Anxiety Workbook: Tips and Strategies to Manage Anxiety, Build Resilience, and Foster Emotional Well-Being

165

6 Yoga Poses for Stress Relief
with the Prisma Pals

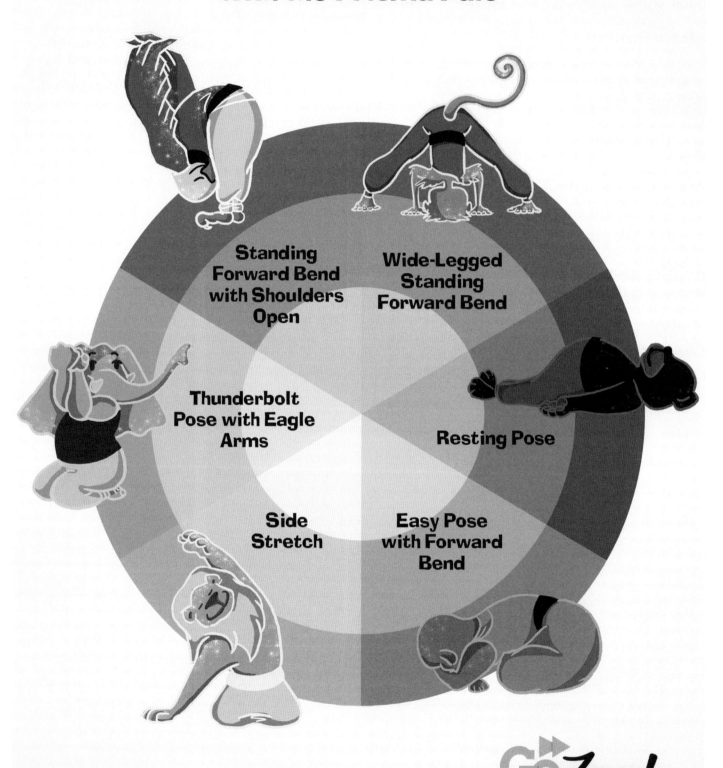

Standing Forward Bend with Shoulders Open

Wide-Legged Standing Forward Bend

Thunderbolt Pose with Eagle Arms

Resting Pose

Side Stretch

Easy Pose with Forward Bend

GoZen!

Source: https://gozen.com/8-yoga-poses-for-stress-relief-for-kids/

Caregiver Information on Performance Anxiety

Understanding and Supporting Your Child's Performance Anxiety

As our children grow and face various challenges in their academic journey, it is essential to recognize that performance anxiety can sometimes be a part of their experience. Performance anxiety is a common condition that arises when students feel excessively worried or nervous about upcoming tests, presentations, or any task that requires them to perform in front of others. As caregivers, understanding this phenomenon and knowing how to support your child is crucial in helping them navigate through their academic endeavors with confidence.

What is Performance Anxiety?

Performance anxiety is a type of stress that affects individuals when they are under pressure to perform well in specific situations. It can manifest at any age including elementary, middle, and high school students. Whether it is giving a speech, taking an exam, or participating in extracurricular activities, performance anxiety can significantly impact a child's academic and social development.

Symptoms of Performance Anxiety

The symptoms of performance anxiety may vary from child to child. Some common indicators caregivers might observe include:

- Restlessness and irritability before the event.
- Physical symptoms like sweating, rapid heartbeat, and upset stomach.
- Negative self-talk, expressing fear of failure, or feeling inadequate.
- Avoidance of situations or activities that trigger anxiety.

Strategies to Support Your Child

- **Create a supportive environment:** Foster an open and non-judgmental atmosphere at home, where your child feels comfortable discussing their fears and concerns without feeling pressured or criticized.
- **Teach relaxation techniques:** Help your child practice relaxation techniques such as deep breathing or mindfulness. These techniques can help calm their nerves before a performance.
- **Encourage balanced preparation:** Emphasize the importance of consistent preparation rather than last-minute cramming. This approach can instill confidence in their abilities and reduce anxiety.
- **Set realistic expectations:** Remind your child that nobody is perfect and that mistakes are a natural part of learning and growing. Encourage a growth mindset, emphasizing progress rather than perfection.
- **Celebrate effort and improvement:** Acknowledge and celebrate your child's hard work and improvement, regardless of the final outcome. This reinforces the idea that their efforts matter more than just the end result.

15-MINUTE FOCUS
Anxiety Workbook: Tips and Strategies to Manage Anxiety, Build Resilience, and Foster Emotional Well-Being

167

Discussion Starters for Conversations with Children

Many children are afraid to talk about their feelings of anxiety. Having a trusted adult initiate the conversation can actually reduce their anxiety. The most effective discussions take place when the child is feeling calm and secure in a comfortable environment. Here are some questions that can help you start conversations with your child about their performance anxiety:

- "I noticed you seemed a little nervous before the presentation. How can I help you feel more at ease next time?"

- "Do you ever feel anxious about tests or performances? It's normal to feel that way sometimes. Let's talk about how we can work through it together."

- "What are some techniques you think might help you relax before a big event? We can try them together."

- "Remember, it's okay to make mistakes. Everyone does. What matters is that you keep trying and learning from them."

- "Is there anything specific you'd like me to do to support you when you have a challenging task ahead?"

As caregivers, your love, understanding, and support are powerful tools in helping your child cope with performance anxiety. By fostering a positive and encouraging environment, you can help your child develop resilience and self-confidence, ensuring that they approach challenges with a sense of empowerment and determination. If you or your child need additional assistance, please reach out to the school counselor for support. We are here to partner with you for your student's success.

168

15-MINUTE FOCUS
Anxiety Workbook: Tips and Strategies to Manage Anxiety, Build Resilience, and Foster Emotional Well-Being

Let's Check-in with Our Students

Taos

Taos's teacher, Mrs. Todd, notices Taos's struggles and decides to implement a supportive approach to help him overcome his performance anxiety. She encourages Taos to participate in smaller, less intimidating group activities, gradually building his confidence. Mrs. Todd also communicates with Taos's family, providing them with resources to support Taos's emotional well-being. Additionally, the school counselor conducts regular sessions with Taos to address his anxiety and develop coping strategies such as relaxation techniques, deep breathing exercises, and positive self-affirmations. She also encourages Taos to participate in the drama club where he can express himself in a more nurturing environment.

With the combined efforts of his teacher, counselor, and family, Taos begins to show signs of improvement. Slowly, he gains confidence in his abilities and his anxiety lessens over time. Taos learns to face his performance anxiety with courage and resilience, paving the way for personal growth and success in the future.

Micah

Ms. Kassidy has seen students struggle with performance anxiety and believes Micah would benefit from additional support. After consulting with the school counselor, Ms. Kassidy introduced mindfulness music exercises in her classes to teach Micah and the rest of her students appropriate skills for managing and reducing anxiety. Ms. Kassidy also offers Micah opportunities to play and record her music individually at school so that she can become comfortable sharing her talent in that setting.

Micah begins meeting with the school counselor to discuss her performance anxiety and learn effective coping strategies. Micah even starts writing a song about her experience struggling with performance anxiety that she hopes will help others. Once Micah's family understands her performance anxiety, they offer unconditional support and encouragement. They started including sets in their musical sessions in which they intentionally made mistakes and have found that it has led to some interesting and surprising creations. Over time, Micah exhibits greater control over her anxiety and a sense of hope of maybe one day sharing her talents with others in person.

15-MINUTE FOCUS
Anxiety Workbook: Tips and Strategies to Manage Anxiety, Build Resilience, and Foster Emotional Well-Being

169

Kessler

Kessler's parents reach out to Coach Browne to share their concerns. Coach Browne proposes they all meet with the school counselor to discuss the situation. The school counselor suggests the added pressure from the recruiters and connecting Kessler's soccer accomplishments to future scholarships and opportunities may have triggered his performance anxiety.

Together with Kessler, the team identifies several interventions to address Kessler's anxiety that include him working individually with the school counselor to learn appropriate coping skills to manage and reduce feelings of anxiety, both on the field and in the classroom. Kessler's parents are going to serve as a filter for recruiters so that Kessler can focus on finding joy in playing soccer again, and the school counselor is going to collaborate with Coach Browne to present a lesson to the whole soccer team on performance anxiety so that all the players can learn what it is and how to prevent it from disrupting their game and life. Kessler is hopeful that these strategies will help him get back on his game, both figuratively and literally.

CHAPTER SIX

School-Wide Supports for Students Experiencing Anxiety

Supporting students struggling with anxiety can be addressed on the individual student level, as a part of the comprehensive school counseling program and/or classroom level, or with a school-wide approach. Typically, individual interventions happen in response to a student who demonstrates a need regarding their ability to manage their anxiety. Similar interventions can be implemented in the school counseling program and classrooms; however, there is also an opportunity to add education and prevention strategies in those approaches. When school leaders decide to adopt a school-wide approach to supporting students with anxiety, they can develop a comprehensive, intentional plan that includes both prevention and intervention strategies developmentally designed to address a broad level of needs represented by the students and adults in the school community.

It is important to note that taking a school-wide approach to supporting students with anxiety begins with education and awareness. It also includes attention to practices and procedures within the school community. A school-wide approach addresses both *what* we do and *how* we do it. This chapter will present activities and strategies for a school-wide approach to supporting students struggling with anxiety through school climate initiatives, behavior and discipline practices, and staff training.

School Climate

Conducting a Values Audit

Much research has been devoted to identifying the link between school culture and student success. That research also shows that a safe and positive school culture increases student achievement and success. Similar studies have shown that the culture of a school is built through practices and policies rooted in the shared values of members of the school community. Understanding those values is a critical step in ensuring that the school climate is one where all students can flourish.

A values audit helps to identify what the school community values in both work and practice. School mission statements often emphasize words like **success** and **achievement**. However, we do not always define those words the same. Accountability measures tend to identify success in terms of percentages—for example,

15-MINUTE FOCUS
Anxiety Workbook: Tips and Strategies to Manage Anxiety, Build Resilience, and Foster Emotional Well-Being

171

the percentage of students that earn a certain score on tests or the percentage of students that graduate. Educators may define success as having the students do their best. Both of those explanations can actually create anxiety in students if they do not know whether their best will also lead to them earning a specific score.

When schools focus on a certain percentage or grade, it can be difficult for students who struggle to reach those thresholds of success. Similarly, when students are encouraged to "do their best," that can also cause anxiety. How do they know what their best is? Students who experience anxiety often cannot determine when they have "done their best." They can push themselves in unhealthy ways because they are not sure what success looks like. Although it might appear that having specific benchmarks of success and encouraging students to give their best effort would reduce anxiety, there are some contradictions in how these play out—and that is the place where anxiety thrives.

A school-wide support for students struggling with anxiety ensures that the school's values and mission are clearly identified, defined, and communicated. It is important to involve various stakeholders in the values audit to ensure that different perspectives are considered. Stakeholders may include administrators, teachers, classified employees, caregivers, students, and district employees who serve the school community. Depending on the size of the school, it may be worthwhile to involve stakeholders via a survey and then establish a smaller internal committee to review and analyze the results. Example survey questions are:

- How does our school define success?
- How is the school's definition of success similar or different from your definition of success for yourself/ your students/your child?
- How is student success recognized or celebrated at our school? Please share examples.
- Please share any positive or negative impacts of recognizing or celebrating success at our school.
- Do you believe all students can achieve success? If not, what students do you believe do not have the opportunity to achieve success?
- How is adult success recognized or celebrated at our school? Please share examples.
- Please share any ideas or suggestions for improving how the school defines success.
- Please share any ideas or suggestions for how the school recognizes or celebrates student success.
- Please share any ideas or suggestions for how the school recognizes or celebrates adult success.

Step 1: Reflect on How Your School Defines Success
- Gather the following documents that often include definitions of success: mission statements, vision statements, school improvement plans, policies for academic recognition, etc.
- Each member of the committee should review these documents and highlight any language that refers to success. Record the highlighted language on a central document/poster.
- Conduct an analysis of the highlighted language together.
- How is the language similar? How is it different?
- What is the underlying message that it sends?
- Based on this language, how might high-achieving students define success?
- How might students that struggle academically define success?
- How might caregivers define success?

Step 2: Review Policies and Examine Actions and Procedures

- Invite members of the committee to walk through the school halls, classrooms, common areas, etc. and look at posters, work that is displayed, bulletin boards, trophy cases, plaques, etc. If outdoor marquees are utilized for messaging, consider reviewing those as well.
- Take pictures of messaging and examples of success. It is important to note that individual student information should not be identified or used. The pictures serve as documentation to help in the analysis of actions and practices around success.
- Collect each committee member's pictures and combine them into one central document or poster. Given the potential number of pictures, utilizing an electronic shared file may be the most efficient way to do this. Categorize or number the pictures to help with the analysis.
- Conduct an analysis of the pictures. Are there other successes being celebrated publicly that may not have been captured in pictures such as school assemblies, announcements on websites, etc.?
- What kinds of success are recognized?
- What types of students are being consistently honored?
- Are there students that are not being recognized?
- What types of student work/skills are being celebrated (academic, athletic, creative talent, citizenship, effort, kindness, leadership, advocacy, responsibility, preparation, perseverance, etc.)?
- How is adult success celebrated in the school?

Step 3: Identify Gaps or Unintended Consequences

- Note any identified gaps between what is recognized as success in Step 2 and the definition of success analyzed in Step 1.
- Are all components that make up the definition of success celebrated in practice?
- Do we celebrate and recognize elements of success that are not reflected in our definition?

You may discover the need to expand your definition of success so that all students can achieve it. You may need to recognize student effort in a more formal way to encourage those students who have a harder time meeting achievement benchmarks.

- As a committee, craft a definition of success that fully represents what success really means to your school community. Consider achievement, effort, and personal/social skills. When all students see ways in which they might be successful, that recognition can reduce their anxiety.
- Identify strategies to recognize and celebrate successes that support the new definition. This may include previous approaches with some adaptations. For example, students who earn high scores on college entrance exams should be celebrated, but so should students who improve their scores from one administration to another. Having an ACT honor wall with photos of students who earn twenty-eight or higher is a good thing. A better thing would be to couple that with a display of students who increased their scores from the first test administration. This communicates that the school values achievement and also values when students work hard to increase their scores, regardless of what that score is.
- New strategies and ideas for recognizing success may also be suggested. A B.U.G. Award could be added to the honors assembly each grading period. B.U.G. stands for Bring Up Grade and it could be given to a student that has worked hard to bring up a grade.

15-MINUTE FOCUS
Anxiety Workbook: Tips and Strategies to Manage Anxiety, Build Resilience, and Foster Emotional Well-Being

173

- Develop a plan to communicate the definition of success and plans to celebrate success to all stakeholders. Do mission statements and branding information need to be adjusted? Will it be communicated as part of school expectations? Or will there be a special messaging campaign about success in our school? Will the committee provide information and resources to faculty and staff about the definition of success and strategies for celebrating it at a faculty meeting or prepare an electronic information file to distribute?

- Determine how often the committee will monitor progress toward alignment of the definition of success with how it is celebrated and recognized. As with any effort, it may be necessary to make adjustments as school needs change or as new information is introduced. Once the initial audit is complete and the plan has been implemented, monitoring progress annually is recommended.

School-Wide Positive Expectations

It is said that we often find what we look for. That rings true in our schools too. Is your student handbook filled with lists of things that students should not do? Are rules communicated in the negative? "Don't talk in the hallway. Don't come into the classroom unprepared. Don't be late to school." These statements communicate that we are looking for inappropriate behavior. For the anxious student, this can send them into great worry. They become so concerned with not doing the wrong thing that they lose sight of what they *should* do.

Constructing rules in the positive sends the message that all students can achieve these expectations. Spending time talking with students about how to meet these expectations helps reduce students' anxiety because they know concretely what they should do. It can also be an investment in instructional time. When students behave appropriately, the teacher does not have to interrupt teaching to correct them. Adopting mantras such as "catch them being good" and "find the good and praise it" can help shift the expectations from "what not to do" to "what to do."

Use the **Positive Student Expectations Worksheet** to evaluate your school's rules and reframe the negative rules into positive expectations.

174

15-MINUTE FOCUS
Anxiety Workbook: Tips and Strategies to Manage Anxiety, Build Resilience, and Foster Emotional Well-Being

NAME:_____

Positive Student Expectations

List school rules that are written in the negative ("Don't do this…").
Reframe them into specific positive behaviors that tells students what is expected of them.

Don't Do This...

 ## Do This...

Ex. Don't come into the classroom unprepared	Come to the class with your book, pencil, and notebook.
Ex. Don't be late to school.	Arrive at school on time ready to begin your learning.

15-MINUTE FOCUS
Anxiety Workbook: Tips and Strategies to Manage Anxiety, Build Resilience, and Foster Emotional Well-Being

175

Morning Meetings and Advisory Meetings

A safe and supportive learning environment is critical to student success. School climate includes both physical and emotional safety. An emotionally safe school is one where a student can feel a sense of belonging and respect, has opportunities to develop healthy relationships, can learn from mistakes without ridicule, and practice skills to enhance their autonomy and agency. Scheduling regular time for activities that create emotionally safe and supportive schools is a proven practice. In elementary school, these are often morning meetings. In middle and high schools, advisory meetings or periods are used for a similar purpose.

When school leaders set the expectations that morning meetings/advisory meetings are going to be a school-wide practice to build and maintain an emotionally safe school climate, it communicates that students' mental wellness is valued and respected. It can reinforce messages that students do have safe spaces and safe people that they can turn to when they are feeling anxious and overwhelmed.

Morning Meetings

(Elementary, Middle, High)

Morning meetings are a school-wide practice developed from the Responsive Classroom model,[23] which is based on the belief that teaching students' social and emotional skills is as important as teaching academic content. Morning meetings can create a **classroom culture** where students feel safe, supported, and ready to learn. This is a great context for all students to learn how to identify triggers of anxiety and how to more effectively manage those feelings before they become excessive and disruptive.

Morning meetings are usually led by the classroom teacher; however, it is not uncommon for a school counselor or administrator to co-lead a morning meaning if it will not upset the dynamics of the group.

As the name suggests, morning meetings are typically held in the morning to begin the school day. The teacher may prefer to hold her meetings later in the day if that fits her schedule better with lunch, special area classes, recess, and other considerations.

Morning meetings will last 20–25 minutes. Often the teacher and students will move their desks/chairs into a circle or sit in a circle on the floor. Consideration should be given to any students who may have physical conditions that prevent them from sitting comfortably on the floor. This should be a safe space that is open and accessible to all students. Although the teacher remains responsible for the room, they can lessen the impact of that imbalance of power by joining the students on the same level that they are sitting in the group (i.e., in a chair or on the floor).

There are four key components to a morning meeting.

- **Greeting:** Students and teachers greet and welcome each other by name.
- **Sharing:** Students share something about themselves or their lives, and the rest of their peers listen, then ask clarifying questions or offer empathetic comments.
- **Activity:** The group participates in a short activity that encourages teamwork that introduces or practices social or academic skills.

- **Morning Message:** Students read a short message from their teacher, usually describing what is to come in the day ahead.

Each of these four components work together to set a **positive tone** for a safe and respectful school environment, preserve a climate of trust, remind students that they are unique and valuable members of the class community, encourage empathy and collaboration, and support social, emotional, and academic learning.

Advisory Periods/Meetings

(Middle, High)

There are multiple models of advisory periods/meetings that middle and high schools utilize to provide academic, social, and emotional support to students. Advisory is usually a shorter period included in the daily schedule. Each day the advisory period may have a different focus, such as receiving academic support, holding club meetings, participating in college and career activities, and delivering social and emotional learning opportunities. The key to successful advisory periods is **establishing clear expectations** for what is to be accomplished during these times and then communicating those expectations with all stakeholders.

As a teacher works with the same group of students every day, they get to know each other and build stronger relationships, which is an attribute of a safe and supportive school culture. Engaging middle and high school students in identifying community expectations for their advisory period is important in developing a space where students feel safe to be themselves and share more honestly about what is important to them. The teacher can facilitate times of sharing and community building by usng the age-appropriate **Discussion Starters for Advisories Handout**.

Like morning meetings, lessons in advisory periods can teach students how to identify triggers that increase their anxiety and learn skills to better manage their feelings of stress and worry to prevent becoming overwhelmed and distressed. When an advisory period is included in a daily schedule, devoting one to two lessons or activities a week to building a safe and supportive school culture is recommended. Specific lessons about anxiety should be delivered throughout the school year, particularly around historically anxiety-inducing events such as the beginning of school, prior to transitions, testing, college application season, before long breaks from school, etc. For students who may need additional support managing their anxiety, school counselors could also provide small group counseling during advisory periods.

For both morning meetings and advisory periods, to ensure that all students receive the same information and message about anxiety it is a good idea to create a series of developmentally appropriate lessons and activities. Identify a few teachers that represent all grade levels in the school to work with the school counselor, school social worker, or other mental health provider to develop a curriculum plan for anxiety education. Topics should include:

- Defining Anxiety
- Recognizing Anxiety and Asking for Help
- Test Anxiety
- Breathing Techniques

15-MINUTE FOCUS
Anxiety Workbook: Tips and Strategies to Manage Anxiety, Build Resilience, and Foster Emotional Well-Being

177

- Mindfulness
- Effective Coping Strategies
- Defining Success

Lessons and activities can be selected from this workbook, other sources, or the team may choose to create their own.

Additional information about morning meetings can be found at https://www.responsiveclassroom.org. *The Morning Meeting Book* by Roxann Kriete and Carol Davis, 3rd edition is an excellent resource.

178

15-MINUTE FOCUS
Anxiety Workbook: Tips and Strategies to Manage Anxiety, Build Resilience, and Foster Emotional Well-Being

Discussion Starters for Advisory

- ☐ When your homework gets hard for you, what do you do?
- ☐ What five words describe you best?
- ☐ What is the most challenging part of school for you?
- ☐ What is the most fun part of school for you?
- ☐ Pretend you are famous. What do you think you would be known for?
- ☐ What is the best school assignment you have ever had?
- ☐ Think about a teacher you really like. What is one thing they said or did that made a difference for you?
- ☐ What is the place where you feel most yourself?
- ☐ If you could travel back in time three years, what advice would you give yourself?
- ☐ If you could make one rule that everyone in the world had to follow, what would it be? Why?
- ☐ If you had a superpower, what would it be?
- ☐ Where is your favorite place to study?
- ☐ What is your secret to getting ready for a quiz or test?
- ☐ If you get a disappointing grade, what do you do?
- ☐ What does a typical weekday morning look like for you?
- ☐ How do you wind down at the end of the day?
- ☐ How well do you sleep?
- ☐ What do you see yourself doing one month after high school? One year after high school?
- ☐ What is one job that really interests you?
- ☐ Is there an app you hate but still use anyway?
- ☐ Do you think of yourself as cautious or as a risk-taker?
- ☐ Share a time when you felt creative.
- ☐ Tell me the story of your name. Where did it come from?
- ☐ Share one person who has inspired you.
- ☐ What motivates you?

- ☐ What is one quality that bothers you about yourself?
- ☐ What is one thing you like about yourself?
- ☐ What is your favorite quality to have in a friend?
- ☐ What is one thing that scares you?
- ☐ If you could trade places with anyone for a day, who would it be and why?
- ☐ What is your biggest pet peeve?
- ☐ Who is your biggest fan?
- ☐ When do you feel most comfortable raising your hand?
- ☐ If you did not finish your homework, what is most likely the reason?
- ☐ What is your favorite thing to do with your family?
- ☐ Talk about a funny or scary adventure you had with a friend.
- ☐ Which do you like better: having specific plans or going with the flow?
- ☐ What is one issue that is really important to you?
- ☐ What is the last great video you watched?
- ☐ If you could live anywhere, where would it be?
- ☐ What is one thing you know how to do that you could teach to others?
- ☐ What five things would you take to a deserted island?
- ☐ At what age should a person be considered an adult?
- ☐ What is something about yourself you could totally brag about but usually do not?
- ☐ You can either leave your hometown forever or never leave your hometown. Which do you choose?
- ☐ What is an unwritten rule about school that everyone knows?
- ☐ What is the best decision you ever made?
- ☐ Your friends are not getting along; how do you try to help them?
- ☐ What advice would you give someone about school?
- ☐ Tell me something you want me to know about you.

15-MINUTE FOCUS
Anxiety Workbook: Tips and Strategies to Manage Anxiety, Build Resilience, and Foster Emotional Well-Being

179

Training

Education and awareness are important when supporting students who struggle with anxiety. The following training agendas include pertinent topics to address with each audience. These trainings can be delivered in a one-day workshop format. They could also be divided into shorter mini lessons to be delivered as a part of regular faculty/staff meetings, grade level meetings, or caregiver meetings. Although in-person or virtual training allows for discussions and questions, the information identified in the training agendas can be disseminated through emails and newsletters. In those instances, include instructions or contact information for readers who may have additional questions.

Training Agenda for Faculty

What is Anxiety?

- Define anxiety
- Discuss signs and symptoms
- Explain brain science of anxiety
- Describe Fight, Flight, Freeze, Fawn Response

Anxiety or Misbehavior

- Discuss similarities between anxiety and misbehavior
- Factors to consider when determining appropriate interventions
- Case Study practice

School-Wide Approaches to Support Students with Anxiety

- Building a Positive School Climate
  - Positive Expectations
  - Behavior Reflections
  - Morning Meeting/Advisory Period
- Defining Success
- Values Audit

Classroom Interventions

- Strategies for teachers
  - Student Interest Surveys
  - Creating Connections
- Classroom Lessons

School Supports

- Mental Health Personnel

Anxiety Workbook: Tips and Strategies to Manage Anxiety, Build Resilience, and Foster Emotional Well-Being

- School Counselor
- School Social Worker
- School Psychologist
- Community Mental Health Provider
- Discuss and differentiate roles, responsibilities, and services
- Referral pathways

Training Agenda for Caregivers

What is Anxiety?
- Define anxiety
- Discuss signs and symptoms
- Explain brain science of anxiety
- Describe Fight, Flight, Freeze, Fawn Response

Supporting Students at Home
- Helping their child understand their anxiety
- Creating personal safety plans with child
- Practicing healthy stress management skills
- Recognizing the roles of nutrition, exercise, and sleep on anxiety

Resources for Additional Support
- School
- Medical
- Community Mental Health

15-MINUTE FOCUS
Anxiety Workbook: Tips and Strategies to Manage Anxiety, Build Resilience, and Foster Emotional Well-Being

181

TRAINING

What is Anxiety?

ADULTS

MATERIALS

- Definition of Anxiety Coloring Sheet (Middle/High)
- What Does Fight, Flight, Freeze, and Fawn Look Like? Handout
- What is Anxiety? Training Assessment
- Colored pencils, markers, or crayons (if desired)

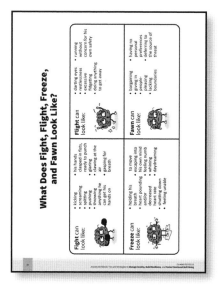

Introduction

Most students and adults have experienced anxiety at some time in their lives. Sometimes anxiety can be helpful. It can push us toward achieving a goal, overcoming a challenge, or avoiding danger. However, for many, anxiety can often become overwhelming and troublesome.

182

15-MINUTE FOCUS
Anxiety Workbook: Tips and Strategies to Manage Anxiety, Build Resilience, and Foster Emotional Well-Being

What is Anxiety?

- Begin the discussion about anxiety.

  How do you define anxiety?

- Allow participants to share answers with the group. Note similarities and differences.

- Introduce definition of anxiety on presentation, poster, or the **Definition of Anxiety Coloring Sheet (Middle/High)**. Pass out the **colored pencils, markers, or crayons** to color the coloring sheet, if desired.

  Anxiety is the excessive concern about a potential triggering event or perceived threat to one's safety. That safety can be physical, emotional, or social.

- Compare answers of the group to the definition. Highlight that the threat or triggering event does not have to be real or defined as a threat by an onlooker. If the person experiencing the event deems that it is a threat, they are likely going to experience anxiety.

Fear vs. Anxiety

- Begin discussion on the relationship between fear and anxiety.

  Often anxiety is associated with fear, but there is a distinct difference between the two.

  Fear is an emotional response to a triggering event.

  Anxiety is the worry about or anticipation of the triggering event.

  For example, a loud storm may elicit fear when thunder strikes. However, worrying about thunder striking when it is raining is anxiety.

15-MINUTE FOCUS
Anxiety Workbook: Tips and Strategies to Manage Anxiety, Build Resilience, and Foster Emotional Well-Being

183

Fight, Flight, Freeze, Fawn Response

- Discuss acute stress response process of Fight, Flight, Freeze, Fawn

  *Anxiety is a physiological response to a perceived threat in the environment. That response prepares the body to protect itself from danger by fighting, fleeing, fawning, or not moving at all. This acute stress response is more commonly known as the **Fight, Flight, Freeze, or Fawn response**.*

  When a person is in danger, they often must act quickly to protect themselves. The brain notices a trigger and determines whether it is a threat.

  *When the **amygdala** (the part of the brain responsible for processing emotions) reacts to the threat, it activates the sympathetic nervous system by releasing hormones that include adrenaline and noradrenaline.*

  *These **hormones** communicate to the body's other systems that they need to stop and focus on the immediate situation. That hormonal release increases the heart rate, blood pressure, and breathing. These changes in the body's homeostasis let those systems know they will have to work effectively and efficiently to find or create a safe environment.*

  - ***Fight**: face the danger and fight the threat aggressively.*
  - ***Flight:** run away from the threat to try and save yourself.*
  - ***Freeze:** do not move/hide in hopes of being ignored until the threat passes.*
  - ***Fawn:** submit to/bargain with the threat in hopes of avoiding conflict.*

  Fawn is seen more in individuals with a history of post-traumatic stress disorder (PTSD) and often reflects a stronger desire to make the person (threat) happier than to take care of oneself.

- Pass out the **What Does Fight, Flight, Freeze, and Fawn Look Like? Handout.** Share what each can look like.

Fight can look like: 	• kicking • screaming • spitting • pushing • throwing anything he can get his hands on	• his hands clasped in fists, ready to punch • glaring • clawing at the air • gasping for breath	**Flight** can look like: 	• darting eyes • restlessness • excessive fidgeting • doing anything to get away	• running without concern for his own safety
Freeze can look like: 	• holding his breath • heart pounding and/or decreased heart rate • shutting down • feeling unable	to move • escaping into his own mind • feeling numb • whining • daydreaming	**Fawn** can look like:	• bargaining • giving in • people-pleasing • lacking boundaries	• having no personal preferences • deferring to the source of threat

15-MINUTE FOCUS
Anxiety Workbook: Tips and Strategies to Manage Anxiety, Build Resilience, and Foster Emotional Well-Being

- Example of the Fight, Flight, Freeze, or Fawn response

  Imagine that you are walking in a public park. As you turn a corner there is a tiger standing on the path in front of you. Your brain has taken in this information and determined this is a potential threat to your physical safety and you feel fear.

  The amygdala, which controls emotions and feelings, takes over and sends stress hormones to your body's other systems, signaling that your body needs protection immediately. As a result, you might:
  - Fight: decide to physically attack the tiger to defend yourself and move to safety.
  - Flight: turn around and run away in the other direction to safety.
  - Freeze: stand very still until the tiger moves away.
  - Fawn: begin talking to the tiger ("nice kitty") and asking it not to eat you for lunch.

  *There are times that if a **threat continues for an extended period** of time, more than one response may be utilized.*

  *Once a threatening situation has been resolved, bodies have to **reset themselves**. Science has shown that after the threat is gone, it takes between twenty to sixty minutes for the body to return to its pre-arousal levels. Requiring students to engage in cognitive activities shortly after an anxiety-inducing event is asking them to do something that they physically cannot do and may even trigger another episode of anxiety.*

  *For people under **acute stress** or with anxiety issues, the sympathetic nervous system is always on guard. The amygdala is hypersensitive and will react to things that others would not recognize as threatening. The FFFF response can happen in the face of imminent physical danger or the result of psychological threats. The response can be triggered due to both **real and imaginary threats**. The amygdala functions unconsciously and almost instantaneously, but that doesn't mean that it is always accurate.*

- Prompt the group with the question below. Give them an opportunity to answer, then share with them the answer.

  What impacts how the brain determines whether something is a threat?

  The answer:
  - ***Knowledge:*** The information we previously have about a potential trigger can help us know whether it is dangerous or not.
  - ***Trauma experiences:*** Research has shown that those who have experienced trauma without therapeutic interventions are more likely to interpret higher levels of threats.
  - ***Previous experiences:*** Similar to knowledge, experiences with a particular trigger can change our perspective on the level of threat a potential trigger poses.
  - ***Risk-taking ability (Pre-Frontal Cortex):*** The pre-frontal cortex does not fully develop until the mid-20s. Executive functioning and assessment of risk are controlled by the pre-frontal cortex.
  - ***Access or Impairment:*** A physical, cognitive, social, or cultural factor that could impact access to determining the level of threat or pathway to safety.

  Consider our example of the tiger in the park. How might the level of threat be impacted if you are:
  - A zookeeper with experience working with big cats.
  - A young child.

15-MINUTE FOCUS
Anxiety Workbook: Tips and Strategies to Manage Anxiety, Build Resilience, and Foster Emotional Well-Being

185

- In a wheelchair.
- Ascribing to the Japanese culture, which believes that the tiger represents strength, courage, and perseverance.
- Continue with this question:

   What are the implications of recognizing that we all may define threats differently?

   We may not always understand or even agree with the reasons someone feels anxiety. However, an important step in helping them to manage their anxiety is recognizing the threat may not be the trigger itself but what the trigger represents.

Wrap Up & Assessment

This can be done verbally, through an exit ticket, electronically (QR code to a survey shared on a presentation slide) or the **What is Anxiety? Training Assessment**.

Answers:
— What is Anxiety? Training Assessment —

What is anxiety?

Answers will vary but look for <u>key words</u> from the definition:
Anxiety is the <u>excessive concern</u> about a <u>potential triggering event or perceived threat</u> to one's <u>safety</u>. That safety can be <u>physical, emotional, or social</u>.

What is the difference between fear and anxiety?

Fear is an emotional response to a triggering event. Anxiety is the worry about or anticipation of the triggering event.

What part of the brain takes over once a trigger has been determined to be a threat?

Amygdala (controls emotions; alerts other systems in the body that it needs protection)

What are the four possible responses to a threat?

Fight: face the danger and fight the threat aggressively.
Flight: run away from the threat to try and save yourself.
Freeze: do not move/hide in hopes being ignored until the threat passes.
Fawn: submit to/bargain with the threat in hopes of avoiding conflict.

How long does your body take to reset once the FFFF response has been triggered?

20–60 minutes before the thinking brain (cognitive functioning) takes over.

Name one factor that influences how the brain determines the level of threat a trigger poses?

One of the following:

- **Knowledge**
- **Pre-Frontal Cortex Development**
- **Previous Experiences**
- **Access/Impairment Conditions**
- **Trauma Experiences**

What is Anxiety?
Training Assessment

What is anxiety?

_____

_____

What is the difference between fear and anxiety?

_____

_____

What part of the brain takes over once a trigger has been determined to be a threat?

_____

What are the four possible responses to a threat?

1. _____

2. _____

3. _____

4. _____

How long does your body take to reset once the FFFF response has been triggered?

_____

_____

Name one factor that influences how the brain determines the level of threat a trigger poses?

_____

_____

Notes or Comments:

_____

_____

_____

_____

15-MINUTE FOCUS
Anxiety Workbook: Tips and Strategies to Manage Anxiety, Build Resilience, and Foster Emotional Well-Being

187

Anxiety vs. Misbehavior Case Study

FACULTY AND STAFF

MATERIALS
- Worried Brain, Distracted Brain Coloring Sheet
- Colored pencils, markers, or crayons (if desired)
- Anxiety vs. Misbehavior Case Study Assessment

This activity can be used with faculty and staff during a faculty meeting or training to help build awareness of ways that anxiety can present as inappropriate behavior. Considerations for how to determine whether the behavior is driven by anxiety and appropriate interventions and supports are suggested.

Introduction

Disruptive behavior can interrupt instruction for all students. It can upset a classroom or school environment and, at times, put student and staff safety in jeopardy. Behaviorists suggest that inappropriate behavior and actions communicate an unmet need. The best way to stop the behavior is to appropriately meet the need. However, that need is not always easy to identify.

Case Study: Mark

- Share the following student scenario:

  Mark is having trouble paying attention in his seventh-grade science class. During the last lab activity, he dropped a beaker and broke it, creating a mess on the floor. When his teacher asks him questions in class, he often responds with "I don't know." Mark frequently visits other lab stations, watching his classmates conduct the experiment rather than completing his own. He consistently forgets to turn in his lab reports. He has received discipline referrals for his behavior, but those consequences do not seem to work. Mark's teacher reviewed his school records and there is no history of similar behaviors.

  Turn to your partner/table and discuss what Mark's behavior may be communicating about his needs.

- Let the groups discuss for 3–5 minutes.

188

15-MINUTE FOCUS
Anxiety Workbook: Tips and Strategies to Manage Anxiety, Build Resilience, and Foster Emotional Well-Being

Share Ideas and Thoughts

- Ask the groups to share their ideas and what factors led to their decisions. You will likely get several different responses. If no one mentions ADHD or anxiety, ask the following probing questions:

  Did anyone think that Mark might have ADHD? What factors led you to that potential explanation?

  Did anyone think that Mark might be suffering from anxiety? What factors led you to that potential explanation?

Anxiety Causes Disruptive Behavior

- Share the following quote on a board, presentation, or the **Worried Brain Distracted Brain Coloring Sheet.** Pass out the **colored pencils, markers, or crayons** to color the coloring sheet, if desired.

  ### *A worried brain is a distracted brain.*

  It is not uncommon for children with serious undiagnosed anxiety to be disruptive at school. They feel the pressure of meeting expectations and fulfilling responsibilities and their anxiety keeps them from handling those stresses constructively. Those behaviors can be misinterpreted as defiant or symptomatic of attention issues.

  Anxiety and ADD can look very much alike. Anxious students find it difficult to avoid distractions and require more time to turn their attention from one task to the next. Being preoccupied with worrisome thoughts and fears can look like not paying attention. However, the student with focus issues may actually be worrying about their safety or the safety of their loved ones. They may also fear getting called on in class and being judged by their classmates and teacher.

- If you have had previous trainings/workshops on anxiety, you may ask participants to identify **behaviors associated with anxiety** that could be misinterpreted as defiant or disruptive.

  Other behaviors associated with anxiety that can be masked as disruptive behaviors:

  - *Mind going blank*
  - *Fatigue from sleep disturbance*
  - *Feeling restless or on edge*
  - *Irritability or acting out*
  - *Fear of talking in front of a group*
  - *Fear of scrutiny or judgment*
  - *Difficulty separating from caregivers*
  - *Avoidance behaviors*
  - *Tantrums or meltdowns*
  - *Headaches, stomachaches, and muscle pains*
  - *Panic attacks*
  - *Excessive worry*

15-MINUTE FOCUS
Anxiety Workbook: Tips and Strategies to Manage Anxiety, Build Resilience, and Foster Emotional Well-Being

189

Evaluating the Case Study: Mark

- Ask partners/tables to discuss:
  - What information do you need to know about Mark to better determine what his actual needs are so that you can provide an appropriate intervention?

- Once groups have had time to discuss, ask them to share their ideas with the larger group. Possible responses:
  - When and where are these behaviors occurring?
    - Is this behavior happening in other classes?
    - Is there a pattern (Mondays, Fridays, etc.)?
  - Is the student experiencing changes?
    - Home/Family/Environment
    - Friends/Social
    - Physical/Health/Sleep (How has Mark been feeling physically?)
  - Are there learning issues?
    - Access to content or assessment of knowledge gained (If the teacher assesses Mark in a different way, is he able to demonstrate mastery/knowledge gained?)
  - Does the student have previous experience with anxiety?
    - If they have experienced anxiety before, what was that like?
    - How did they handle it? Do they have similar feelings now?
    - When Mark gets worried how does he act/handle that?
  - Share these final thoughts:

    An educator is not trained to make a determination about any specific diagnosis; however, they can certainly share concerns with Mark's caregiver. The information gathered can provide a clearer picture of what is driving Mark's inappropriate behavior.

    *It is important to highlight that **disruptive or inappropriate behavior should be addressed**. Sometimes disruptive behavior is just disruptive behavior. However, understanding what is driving these actions will help educators identify effective interventions that can better equip the student to handle their anxiety if that is the root of the issue.*

- Consider a quick review of student **supports** available for students who are demonstrating a need (i.e., school counselor, school social worker, Section 504, RTI2, student support team, etc.) and how to initiate a referral.

190

15-MINUTE FOCUS
Anxiety Workbook: Tips and Strategies to Manage Anxiety, Build Resilience, and Foster Emotional Well-Being

Wrap Up & Assessment

- To conclude the meeting/training share the **Anxiety vs. Misbehavior Case Study Assessment**. This can be done verbally, through an exit ticket, electronically (QR code to a survey shared on a presentation slide) or a follow-up survey.

Answers:
Anxiety vs. Misbehavior Case Study Assessment

A worried brain is a _____ brain.

Answer: Distracted

When a student exhibits disruptive behavior, what are two factors to consider before determining an appropriate intervention?

Answer:

- **When and where are the behaviors occurring**
- **Is the student experiencing changes?**
- **Learning issues**
- **Previous experience with anxiety**

15-MINUTE FOCUS
Anxiety Workbook: Tips and Strategies to Manage Anxiety, Build Resilience, and Foster Emotional Well-Being

191

NAME:_____

Anxiety vs. Misbehavior
Case Study Assessment

A worried brain is a _____ brain.

When a student exhibits disruptive behavior, what are two factors to consider before determining an appropriate intervention?

1. _____

_____

2. _____

_____

Notes or Comments: _____

_____

_____

NAME:_____

Anxiety vs. Misbehavior
Case Study Assessment

A worried brain is a _____ brain.

When a student exhibits disruptive behavior, what are two factors to consider before determining an appropriate intervention?

1. _____

_____

2. _____

_____

Notes or Comments: _____

_____

_____

15-MINUTE FOCUS
Anxiety Workbook: Tips and Strategies to Manage Anxiety, Build Resilience, and Foster Emotional Well-Being

193

Behavior Reflection

(Elementary, Middle, High)

Inappropriate behavior is a language children and adults use when they do not have the words or do not know how to use their words to communicate what they need. Students with anxiety struggle to articulate their feelings or explain their behaviors. Therefore, supporting these students when they are not meeting behavioral or academic expectations is critical to reducing not only unwanted actions but also the anxiety itself.

We must approach these situations with a different lens of discipline so that we can help students regain a sense of control. Unwanted actions do need attention, but before determining what the student's consequence will be, a non-punitive discussion with the student should take place.

If a student's disruptive behavior is part of the Fight, Flight, Freeze, or Fawn response, the amygdala in their brain has taken over and they will need 20 to 60 minutes for their body and mind to reset after the incident before they are able to access cognitive functioning. It may be necessary to give the student quiet time before they are able to discuss or process an incident.

The following age-appropriate **Understanding My Behavior Worksheets** can be completed by the student and then discussed with the teacher, administrator, or school counselor. As an alternative, the questions on the worksheet can be used to facilitate a discussion with the student. These worksheets can help to determine what was driving the disruptive behavior. The worksheets focus on the cause of the behavior rather than processing the incident and learning new skills. Keep in mind that the school counselor should not be involved with determining any type of discipline for a student.

If it is determined that the student is struggling with anxiety and that the anxiety contributed to the inappropriate behavior, it is important to note that we are not suggesting that students with anxiety should not have consequences for their actions. Administrators and teachers are encouraged to consider a broader definition of consequences. In traditional approaches, those consequences were enforced to help students learn not to engage in inappropriate behaviors. However, helping anxious students learn techniques to better manage and reduce their anxiety will lead to longer-lasting results rather than being suspended or having to perform punitive tasks. Consider approaches aligned to restorative justice practices. Include interventions with the school counselor to help the student learn skills to reduce and manage their anxiety.

Understanding My Behavior
Younger Elementary

How was my day going?

GOOD   BAD   OKAY

Before I came to school today, things at home were:

UPSET   CALM   EXCITED

What rule did I break?

_____

_____

Before I broke the rule I was thinking:

_____

_____

_____

_____

Before I broke the rule I was feeling:

_____

_____

_____

_____

I broke the rule because I wanted to:

_____

_____

15-MINUTE FOCUS
Anxiety Workbook: Tips and Strategies to Manage Anxiety, Build Resilience, and Foster Emotional Well-Being

195

Understanding My Behavior
Older Elementary

How was my day going?

_____
_____
_____

Before I came to school today, things at home were:

_____
_____
_____

What rule did I break?

_____
_____

Before I broke the rule I was thinking:

_____
_____
_____
_____
_____

Before I broke the rule I was feeling:

_____
_____
_____
_____

I broke the rule because I wanted to:

_____
_____

Understanding My Behavior
Middle/High

Describe Your Day

ROUTINES	PHYSICAL NEEDS
Did anything out of the ordinary happen? Did you wake up at your usual time? Did you get to school on time?	Did you eat breakfast? Did you have clean clothes for school? Do/Did you have lunch?
ACADEMIC	**SOCIAL**
Did you come to school with your supplies/homework? Do you have any test or projects due today? Did you get any unexpected grades today?	Have you had any conflicts with family or friends?

Describe your inappropriate behavior:

_____

_____

What were you thinking prior to the incident?

_____

_____

What were you feeling prior to the incident?

_____

_____

15-MINUTE FOCUS
Anxiety Workbook: Tips and Strategies to Manage Anxiety, Build Resilience, and Foster Emotional Well-Being

197

Classroom Interventions for Teachers

Every classroom holds a community of learners, and educators know the impact of the positive environment schools provide. Research shows that students can thrive in a safe and supportive learning environment, and schools have worked diligently to create those positive school climates. But when a student experiences anxiety, it impacts their academic achievement, social and emotional development, and college and career readiness. When a student is experiencing anxiety, teachers can use a variety of interventions to help them. Before these strategies can be utilized, the student needs to trust that their teacher understands them and can help. When a teacher is able to build a relationship with a child, they can often help the student use tools to handle anxiety and prevent full-blown anxiety attacks.

- **Communicate with the student and caregiver consistently.** Let them know that you want to help. If you observe changes in the student's behavior, both positive and negative, let the caregiver know. Older students should be included in discussions about how best to get support.

- **Consult with the school counselor to identify helpful strategies** to support the student and determine whether counseling services are needed.

- **Make sure specific adults know the student's triggers and coping strategies.** While all school staff do not need to know the details of the student's situation, it is important that adults who will interact with the student are aware of potential triggers and effective strategies to mediate those triggers. This includes cafeteria staff, bus drivers, school secretary, school nurse, and related arts teachers.

- **Use clear and concise language.** Avoid exaggerations and highly emotional words.

- **Make accommodations when possible.** For example, to prepare for timed tests, practice fun or low-stakes activities with the students so they can get an idea of how much time they will have to complete tests or assessments.

- **Provide as much consistency as possible.** When there are changes in the routine, discuss the changes with the student and make sure that they understand what is supposed to be done.

- **Focus on effort rather than perfection.** When discussing academic progress, start with what the student did well.

- **Choose collaborative groups intentionally.** Avoid pairing the anxious child with a perfectionist or high achiever. That can create more pressure for the student.

- **Create safe spaces/zones, calm down spaces, etc. in your room.** Refer to **Setting Up a Calm Corner in Your Classroom** for suggestions and ideas. Make sure the procedures for accessing those spaces are clear for all children. When is it appropriate to use them? Does the student need to ask permission or just move to that part of the classroom? What kinds of activities are appropriate for that space? How long can a student stay there? Can there be more than one student there at a time?

Student Interest Survey

(Elementary, Middle, High)

Below you will find two age-appropriate **Student Interest Surveys** designed to help you understand what makes your students nervous and what helps them feel safe. Asking these questions will build trust as you begin to integrate the **Classroom Interventions to Support Students Experiencing Anxiety** (see handout). These interventions provide support through school routines, learning and assessments, and personal and emotional needs. These can be utilized for short periods of time or may need to be in place throughout the school year. It is important to regularly discuss the student's needs and the effectiveness of the interventions so that adjustments can be made. As the student learns to successfully manage their anxiety, they may elect to discontinue using some interventions.

15-MINUTE FOCUS
Anxiety Workbook: Tips and Strategies to Manage Anxiety, Build Resilience, and Foster Emotional Well-Being

199

ELEMENTARY
•STUDENT INTEREST SURVEY•

NAME: _____

I'M REALLY GOOD AT:

I WANT TO LEARN:

SOMETHING THAT
MAKES ME NERVOUS:

SOMETHING THAT
MAKES ME FEEL SAFE:

TALKING IN FRONT OF
CLASS MAKES ME FEEL:

I LIKE BEING RECOGNIZED FOR GOOD WORK OR EFFORT:

☐ IN PRIVATE   ☐ IN FRONT OF THE CLASS   ☐ IN PUBLIC

I LIKE MY WORK BEING DISPLAYED:

☐ IN THE CLASSROOM   ☐ IN THE HALLWAY   ☐ NEVER PUBLICLY

200

15-MINUTE FOCUS
Anxiety Workbook: Tips and Strategies to Manage Anxiety, Build Resilience, and Foster Emotional Well-Being

Student Interest Survey

MIDDLE/HIGH

Name: _____

I want to learn:

_____

_____

_____

I'm really good at:

_____

_____

_____

_____

Something that makes me nervous:

_____

_____

Talking in front of class makes me feel:

_____

_____

_____

Something that makes me feel safe:

_____

_____

_____

I like being recognized for good work or effort:

☐ in private   ☐ in front of the class   ☐ in public

I like my work being displayed:

☐ in the classroom   ☐ in the hallway   ☐ never publicly

15-MINUTE FOCUS
Anxiety Workbook: Tips and Strategies to Manage Anxiety, Build Resilience, and Foster Emotional Well-Being

201

Classroom Interventions to Support Students Experiencing Anxiety

Elementary, Middle, High

SCHOOL ROUTINES	LEARNING & ASSESSMENTS	PERSONAL & EMOTIONAL
Extra time and warnings before transitions	Frequent check-ins for understanding	Cool-down passes to take a break from the classroom
Preferential seating (near the door, the front of the room, the teacher's desk, the back of the room)	Not requiring read aloud or work at the board in front of the class	Identify at least one adult besides teacher/counselor that the student can seek help from when feeling anxious
Clearly stated and written expectations (behavior and academic)	Videotaped presentations or presenting in front of the teacher instead of the whole class	Establishing a signal for the student to let the teacher know that they need to take a few moments at their desk to disengage
Preferential group with teacher/adult the student knows for field trips	Extended time for tests	Incorporate mindfulness activities into the classroom activities to benefit all students
Preferential seating in large assemblies near the back of the room	Tests taken in a separate, quiet environment to reduce performance pressure and distraction	Implement Morning Meetings/Community Circles
Pair student with a peer to assist with transitions to lunch, recess, and other activities outside the classroom	Breaking down assignments/tests into smaller sections	
When possible, let the child or family know when a substitute will be in the classroom can help the child prepare	Word banks and equation sheets on tests	
	Modified tests and homework	
	Set reasonable time limits for homework	
	Record class lectures or make copy of lecture notes	

Building Authentic Connections

(Elementary, Middle, High)

Students experiencing anxiety feel that their safety is threatened. Safe relationships and spaces can be a protective factor and reduce those anxious feelings. Students are more inclined to trust their teachers with their tender emotions when they have relationships with them that are built with authentic connections. Building these relationships takes time and intention; however, research has shown that it is an investment in the classroom culture that benefits all students.

Greeting Students

When students arrive to your class, make a point of greeting them every day. Developing a creative welcome for each student, such as handshake, signal, or gesture, that tells the student that you know who they are. This can be powerful for children who may feel unseen or unknown.

Knowing Students' Talents

Students have many talents and skills, some of which are not measured on an academic assessment. When a teacher recognizes a student for a talent or skill unrelated to the academic content of the class, the student feels acknowledged, it expands the definition of success for all, and the student is empowered to use that skill in a positive way.

One Thing

An open line of communication is key for maintaining safe and supportive relationships. A regular practice that can be included with all tests and quizzes is asking students to share "One Thing I Wish My Teacher Knew" on the back of their papers before turning them in. Instruct students that they can share anything they want, such as their favorite food, plans for the weekend, or how well they think they did on the test. They can also share more personal things such as problems at with friends, issues at home, or if they did not understand something about the content being tested. The teacher can follow up with the students as necessary.

Sharing Mutual Trust

Trusting someone can be risky. Showing students that you are willing to trust them will show them that they can put their trust in you. Sharing appropriate personal information about your likes, dislikes, fears, hopes, dreams, disappointments, and how you have overcome challenges can tell students that just as you trust part of you with them, they can trust part of themselves with you.

Connect Learning to Students World

Students are more engaged in learning when it is more relevant to their world. For teachers to connect the course content to meaningful aspects of students' lives, they should know what is important to them. This includes knowing their cultural, social media, music, art, technology, and entertainment world. It can be daunting to keep up with ever-changing interests. Setting aside time to ask students what is relevant can help. Not all students are alike, so make sure that you get feedback from all students. Keep in mind that

15-MINUTE FOCUS
Anxiety Workbook: Tips and Strategies to Manage Anxiety, Build Resilience, and Foster Emotional Well-Being

203

connecting learning to students' world is not limited to content. Consider the instructional methods that will engage students. For example, if unsolved true crime genres are popular, consider presenting a science lesson in a similar format.

Be Consistent

An important way to build trust in relationships is to be consistent in what we say and do. Students will watch to see if we follow through with what we tell them we are going to do. They will also watch to see if we treat them the same way that we treat others. They want to know that they matter as much as any other student in the classroom. Most students understand that there are fellow classmates that have different needs that should be addressed in varied ways. However, whether they are able to articulate it or not, students recognize when they see inequity in the classroom. That inequity will likely work against any efforts to build trusting relationships.

Individual Attention

Time and attention are important in building and maintaining trusting relationships. Although time is a resource in short supply for teachers, when they can spend two minutes with each student once a week they are investing in their academic achievement as well as their connection with the student. Formally or informally checking in with each student allows the teacher to identify whether there are any challenges the student is facing academically, socially, or personally. These check-ins provide the student with an opportunity to share feedback with the teacher about their learning, concerns, or accomplishments.

Additional Resources

There are many other resources for developing positive connections with students. Specifically, Amie Dean's *Behavior Interventions: Your Roadmap for Creating a Positive Classroom Community*,[24] is an excellent workbook filled with numerous strategies for building a safe and supporting learning environment. Students struggling with anxiety will benefit from the activities and interventions Amie shares. Another great resource is Hal Urban's *Lessons from the Classroom: 20 Things Good Teachers Do*,[25] which includes techniques and strategies to create positive classroom climates. Finally, there is the Office of the State Superintendent of Education (OSSE) curated best practices for developing a supportive learning environment. Their resource *Relationship-Building Strategies for the Classroom*,[26] outlines ten specific in-person and virtual activities teachers can utilize to strengthen connections with their students.

204

15-MINUTE FOCUS
Anxiety Workbook: Tips and Strategies to Manage Anxiety, Build Resilience, and Foster Emotional Well-Being

Setting Up a Calm Corner in Your Classroom

A Calm Corner is a designated area of the classroom where students can go when they are feeling big emotions and need time and space to reset. Utilizing a Calm Corner serves as a strategy to empower students to manage their emotions and behaviors. When students are experiencing anxiety, they often seek a safe space. A Calm Corner can provide a sense of safety and reduce their anxious feelings. Calm corners also reinforce the idea that everyone experiences overwhelming feelings and normalizes taking a break to reset as an effective coping skill.

Creating A Calm Corner

- **Select a space in the classroom separate from the regular learning area.** Try to choose a place that will have limited distractions. The teacher should be able to supervise the student while they are in the Calm Corner.

- **Provide a comfortable place for your students to sit**. A bean bag, pillow, rug, bathmat, or small weighed blanket can create a relaxing space. Weighted blankets have been shown to have a calming effect for those feeling anxious.

- **Put small squeeze toys, fidgets, or tactile objects in a basket** for students to students to squeeze, play with, or hold. Squeezing or manipulating something can help to release tension in the body and release endorphins which can work to reduce anxiety.

- **Post visual reminders of coping skills** that they can use specifically in the Calm Corner. These can be made during class activities and created by students. Seeing their own work in their Calm Corner can remind them of their own power and strength.

- **Provide coloring pages.** Coloring gives students a way to express their emotions.

- **Consider letting students listen to music with headphones** in the Calm Corner. Music can be very calming, even if the student's choice of music may not seem calm to adults.

- **Add an exercise or yoga mat,** if your space is large enough. Exercise can be an effective coping skill. A student could do some simple exercises such as sit ups, push-ups, or stretching to help them reset.

Setting Expectations for the Calm Corner

- **Discuss the purpose of the Calm Corner with the students.** Reinforce that it is not a punishment and is available for everyone.

- **Explain when and how the students can use the Calm Corner.** Is there any time when they cannot go to the Calm Corner? (during a test/standardized test/when someone else is there/etc.)

- **Let the students know how long they can stay there and how to signal you if they need more time.** Consider using a sand timer.

- **Identify what behaviors are safe or unsafe** in the space.

- **Check-in with the students** to see how the Calm Corner is working for them and adjust as needed.

15-MINUTE FOCUS
Anxiety Workbook: Tips and Strategies to Manage Anxiety, Build Resilience, and Foster Emotional Well-Being

205

Final Thoughts

Student success is the ultimate goal for educators. Just as we know that success can mean different things for each student, we must also acknowledge that the path they take through their education can also be different. Every child comes to school with their own unique experiences and capacity for learning. Students struggling with anxiety can have their journey derailed. They need the support of caring adults to teach them more about what they are experiencing and empower them to use appropriate coping skills to manage and reduce their anxiety. Thank you for being one of those caring adults. When you apply the knowledge, strategies, and skills presented in this workbook, you are helping students move toward success. Whether you are counseling an individual student, teaching students how to recognize their anxiety triggers, or collaborating with stakeholders to create a more supportive learning environment, know I am cheering you and your students on!

Dr. Leigh

DOWNLOADABLE RESOURCES AND TEMPLATES

Please visit **15minutefocusseries.com** and click Downloadable Resources. Enter the code below in the form to download the file to your device.

ANXWorkbook517

206

15-MINUTE FOCUS
Anxiety Workbook: Tips and Strategies to Manage Anxiety, Build Resilience, and Foster Emotional Well-Being

Notes

1. Bagwell, L. (2021). *15-Minute Focus: Anxiety: Worry, Stress, and Fear.* National Center for Youth Issues.

2. Cripps, Danielle. (2019). Exploring the effectiveness of a school-based gratitude intervention on children's levels of anxiety, sense of school belonging and sleep quality. (Doctoral Thesis, University of Southampton), 142pp.

3. Center for Behavioral Health Research. (2023). Mapping the landscape of mental health services and resources for K-12 students in Tennessee.

4. Herzig-Anderson, K., Colognori, D., Fox, J. K., Stewart, C. E., & Warner, C. M. (2012). School-based anxiety treatments for children and adolescents. *Child and Adolescent Psychiatric Clinics*, 21(3), 655-668.

5. Cleveland Clinic https://my.clevelandclinic.org/health/symptoms/23154-neurodivergent

6. Reimherr, F. W., Marchant, B. K., Gift, T. E., & Steans, T. A. (2017). ADHD and anxiety: clinical significance and treatment implications. *Current Psychiatry Reports*, 19, 1-10.

7. Tsang T. W., Kohn M. R., Clarke S. D., Williams L. M., Efron D., Clark C. R., Lamb C. (2015). Anxiety in Young People With ADHD: Clinical and Self-Report Outcomes. *Journal of Attention Disorders*, 19(1), 18–26. https://doi.org/10.1177/1087054712446830

8. Sciberras, E., Mulraney, M., Anderson, V., Rapee, R. M., Nicholson, J. M., Efron, D., Lee, K., Markopoulos, Z., & Hiscock, H. (2018). Managing Anxiety in Children With ADHD Using Cognitive Behavioral Therapy: A Pilot Randomized Controlled Trial. *Journal of Attention Disorders*, 22(5), 515–520.

9. Bishop, C., Mulraney, M., Rinehart, N., & Sciberras, E. (2019). An examination of the association between anxiety and social functioning in youth with ADHD: A systematic review. *Psychiatry Research*, 273, 402-421.

10. Liu, T.-L., Hsiao, R. C., Chou, W.-J., & Yen, C.-F. (2021). Social Anxiety in Victimization and Perpetration of Cyberbullying and Traditional Bullying in Adolescents with Autism Spectrum Disorder and Attention Deficit/Hyperactivity Disorder. *International Journal of Environmental Research and Public Health*, 18(11), 5728.

11. Hallett, V., Lecavalier, L., Sukhodolsky, D. G., Cipriano, N., Aman, M. G., McCracken, J. T.,... & Scahill, L. (2013). Exploring the manifestations of anxiety in children with autism spectrum disorders. *Journal of Autism and Developmental Disorders*, 43, 2341-2352.

12. Wijnhoven, L. A., Creemers, D. H., Vermulst, A. A., & Granic, I. (2018). Prevalence and risk factors of anxiety in a clinical Dutch sample of children with an autism spectrum disorder. *Frontiers in Psychiatry*, 9, 50.

13. McMahon, E. M., Corcoran, P., O'Regan, G., Keeley, H., Cannon, M., Carli, V.,... & Wasserman, D. (2017). Physical activity in European adolescents and associations with anxiety, depression and well-being. *European Child & Adolescent Psychiatry*, 26, 111-122.

14. Lewis, H. (2021). A Safe Place to Land: Music classes as havens for anxious and other youth. *The Canadian Music Educator*, 62(4), 35-40.

15. Hoge, E. A., Bui, E., Marques, L., Metcalf, C. A., Morris, L. K., Robinaugh, D. J., … Simon, N. M. (2013). Randomized Controlled Trial of Mindfulness Meditation for Generalized Anxiety Disorder: Effects on Anxiety and Stress Reactivity. *The Journal of Clinical Psychiatry*, 74(8), 786–792.

16. Husabo, E., Haugland, B. S., McLeod, B. D., Baste, V., Haaland, Å. T., Bjaastad, J. F.,... & Wergeland, G. J. (2021). Treatment fidelity in brief versus standard-length school-based interventions for youth with anxiety. *School Mental Health*, 1-14.

17. Hylton, E., Malley, A., & Ironson, G. (2019). Improvements in adolescent mental health and positive affect using creative arts therapy after a school shooting: A pilot study. *The Arts in Psychotherapy*, 65, 101586.

18. Thielemann, J. F. B., Kasparik, B., König, J., Unterhitzenberger, J., & Rosner, R. (2022). A systematic review and meta-analysis of trauma-focused cognitive behavioral therapy for children and adolescents. *Child abuse & Neglect*, 134, 105899.

19. Cimolai, V., Schmitz, J., & Sood, A. B. (2021). Correction to: effects of mass shootings on the mental health of children and adolescents. *Current Psychiatry Reports*, 23, 1-1.

20. Upton, C. C., Diambra, J. F., Brott, P. E., & Budesa, Z. (2023). Photography as a Wellness Tool for Counselors-in-Training. *Journal of Educational Research and Practice*, 13(1), 1.

21. Liu, T. L., Hsiao, R. C., Chou, W. J., & Yen, C. F. (2021). Social anxiety in victimization and perpetration of cyberbullying and traditional bullying in adolescents with autism spectrum disorder and attention deficit/hyperactivity disorder. *International journal of environmental research and public health*, 18(11), 5728.

22. Cripps, D. (2019). Exploring the effectiveness of a school-based gratitude intervention on children's levels of anxiety, sense of school belonging and sleep quality (Doctoral dissertation, University of Southampton).

23. https://www.edutopia.org/practice/morning-meetings-creating-safe-space-learning

24. Dean, A. (2023) *Behavior Interventions: Your Roadmap for Creating a Positive Classroom Community.* National Center for Youth Issues, TN

25. Urban, H. (2008). *Lessons from the Classroom: 20 Things Good Teachers Do.* Great Lessons Press, NY.

26. Office of the State Superintendent of Education. (2022). Relationship-Building Strategies for the Classroom. https://osse.dc.gov/sites/default/files/dc/sites/osse/page_content/attachments/Relationhip_Building_Toolkit.pdf

15-MINUTE FOCUS
Anxiety Workbook: Tips and Strategies to Manage Anxiety, Build Resilience, and Foster Emotional Well-Being

207

Acknowledgments

To complete a project of this nature requires much more than a singular effort. Were it not for the dreams, encouragement, sharing, patience, and sacrifice of many this book would not exist.

To my family and friends, thank you for your continued encouragement and belief in my dream to be a beacon of support for school counselors.

To Jennifer, thank you for sharing your dreams with me. I love our conversations that begin with you saying, "What do you think about…?" Thank you for connecting my words with a talented team that transformed them into this beautiful book. I appreciate you more than you know.

To the school counseling community, thank you for being my tribe and my professional home. Your challenges and celebrations inspire me. I continue to be humbled by your unwavering commitment to your students. You are a gift to your students, and I will always be your loudest cheerleader!

To my handsome and brave nephews, GB and BB, you remain my inspiration for this work. You are navigating an educational experience that is far different than I had. My deepest desire is for you to enjoy the opportunity to grow, learn, and become who you fully are in a safe and supportive environment. I am your biggest fan!

To Riley and Cooper, you endured many long days and nights curled up at your mom's side while she worked. You were always ready for snuggles and kisses though, reminding me that in the end, unconditional love and support is truly the best gift. Love you most!

208

15-MINUTE FOCUS
Anxiety Workbook: Tips and Strategies to Manage Anxiety, Build Resilience, and Foster Emotional Well-Being

About the Author

DR. LEIGH BAGWELL is a member of the School Counseling Core Faculty in the School of Social and Behavioral Sciences at Capella University. Bagwell joined Capella in the spring of 2022 shortly after completing her doctorate in Counselor Education and Supervision from the University of Tennessee. She began her career as an elementary and middle school counselor before moving to leadership and supervisory roles in school counseling for preK-12 education in both urban and suburban school districts then ultimately serving as the Director of School Counseling Services for the Tennessee Department of Education. As a school counseling educator and leader, her mission is to provide school counselors and administrators with the training and resources needed to deliver high quality, student driven, data informed comprehensive school counseling programs to all students. She believes that when school counselors and school leaders work together, all students can have have access to the opportunities and supports they need to successfully move through their elementary, secondary, and postsecondary education into their chosen career.

In addition to her work in Tennessee, Bagwell partners with school counselors and school counseling leaders throughout the country using her experiences and knowledge to build their capacity to more effectively serve students. She has authored multiple books in the 15 Minute Focus Series – *Anxiety: Worry, Stress, and Fear* and an accompanying workbook, along with *Self-Harm and Self-Injury: When Emotional Pain Becomes Physical*, and has served as a consultant on several SEL children's books. She has conducted research on mental health supports for students and families and is a consultant with an international organization developing tools and materials that help school counselors deliver effective school counseling programs to all students. Dr. Bagwell's hope is to equip and empower school counselors to use their unique knowledge and skills to advocate and support all students to reach their potential and achieve their dreams.

15-MINUTE FOCUS
Anxiety Workbook: Tips and Strategies to Manage Anxiety, Build Resilience, and Foster Emotional Well-Being

209

Also available from Leigh Bagwell

15-Minute Focus: Anxiety

Worry, Stress, and Fear

Learn the physiological progression from a trigger to a full-blown anxiety attack and gain a variety of prevention and intervention strategies. Readers will get a clarification of anxiety vs. misbehavior, along with a breakdown of various anxiety disorders and how they present.

15-Minute Focus: Self-Harm and Self-Injury

When Emotional Pain Becomes Physical

Dr. Bagwell offers an in-depth look at the who, what, and why of self-harm (nonsuicidal self-injury-NSSI). You will discover types of NSSI behavior, the relationship between self-harm and suicidal ideation, and signs and symptoms of NSSI beyond wounds and scars.

210

15-MINUTE FOCUS
Anxiety Workbook: Tips and Strategies to Manage Anxiety, Build Resilience, and Foster Emotional Well-Being

A Brief Look at Leigh's Workshops

MTSS and School Counseling: Maximizing Supports for Student Success

School counselors work to provide data-driven, evidence-based school counseling programs to impact student achievement, social and personal competencies, and college and career readiness. Multi-Tiered Systems of Support (MTSS) is a research-based framework for addressing student needs through effective prevention and intervention strategies. MTSS has been successfully applied to both academic skills and the positive behavior of all students. Traditionally, school counselors have played an important role in these efforts to advocate and serve students; however, the comprehensive school counseling program (CSCP) has not always been identified as a support for the MTSS model. What if school counselors could align their CSCP to the MTSS framework? Let's explore how connecting these two models will help maximize the effectiveness and efficiency of school counselors, provide more meaningful support to students, and advocate for the many ways that school counselors impact student growth, development, and success.

Support Students Struggling with Anxiety and Stress

Anxiety and stress can cause students to feel isolated and overwhelmed, preventing them from learning in the classroom. When students experience anxiety and stress, they need help navigating through it. Rather than tell our students not to worry, our job as educators is to recognize when students are experiencing anxiety and get them the support they need. During this session we will discuss the physiology of anxiety, signs that a student may be in distress, and specific interventions educators can employ to support their students. We will also highlight steps schools can take to prevent an anxious and stressful learning environment. Working together, educators can become powerful advocates for students struggling with anxiety so that they can thrive in the classroom and in life.

Social and Emotional Learning

Our emotions and relationships affect how and what we learn and how we use what we learn in school, work, family, and community contexts. As many schools and districts integrate social and emotional learning frameworks into their classroom instruction, services provided by student support staff can be especially effective in promoting the school success of children who have social, emotional, and mental health problems that interfere with learning. During this session participants will discuss the specific role of school counselors, school social workers, school psychologists, school nurses and other student support professionals in supporting the social and emotional learning initiatives that lead to student success.

15-MINUTE FOCUS
Anxiety Workbook: Tips and Strategies to Manage Anxiety, Build Resilience, and Foster Emotional Well-Being

211

Integrating Social and Emotional Learning with Career Development to Prepare College and Career Ready Students.

When preparing students for success in postsecondary education and the workforce it is important that they have academic and content knowledge and training. College and career readiness begins with early exposure and awareness to a broad range of career fields and employability skills. It also includes helping students connect what they are learning in the classroom to their dreams and future career goals. Another important component of college and career readiness is social and emotional development. Self-awareness, self-management and interpersonal skills are critical to students' transition to postsecondary and the workforce.

College and career readiness continues to focus on the development and refinement of both academic and social emotional skills. It also broadens the scope from just knowing about different careers to exploring the high demand opportunities in their communities, aligning personal interests and aptitudes to career fields, and identifying specific pathways to move successfully from secondary to postsecondary to the workforce. These skills will not only prepare them for success in the workplace, but also success in both secondary and postsecondary education.

Because school counseling programs integrate academic preparation, social and emotional development with college and career readiness, school counselors are uniquely positioned to lead this important work. It begins by ensuring that school counselors have strategies and practices that will deepen their students' understanding of the world of work and connect it to their school and life experiences. School counselors will increase their capacity to provide high quality school counseling services and support students as they move along their chosen pathways to and through secondary and postsecondary education and on to the workforce.

College and Career Readiness: K(indergarten) to J(ob) *K-12 Session*

What does a successful student look like? What are the skills, knowledge, and experiences our students need to transition effectively from education and training to the workforce? Preparing today's students for tomorrow's workforce goes beyond the traditional career speakers and "careers on wheels" of days past. More than half of our students will pursue a career that has not been developed yet. College and career readiness begins with early exposure and awareness to a broad range of career fields and employability skills. These skills will not only prepare them for success in the workplace, but also success in both secondary and postsecondary education. When students transition from elementary schools to middle and high schools, they also progress from career awareness to career exploration and planning. College and career readiness continues to focus on the development and refinement of employability skills. It also broadens the scope from just knowing about different careers to exploring the high demand opportunities in their communities, aligning personal interests and aptitudes to career fields, and identifying specific pathways to move successfully from secondary to postsecondary to the workforce.

Using school counseling standards as the foundation, we will discuss the profile of a college and career ready student. Participants will leave with specific school counseling strategies and practices that will deepen their students' understanding of the world of work and connect it to their school experience. School counselors will increase their capacity to provide high quality advising and support students as they move along their chosen pathways to and through secondary and postsecondary education and on to the workforce.

15-minute focus
Brief Counseling Techniques that Work

Look for these books in the series!

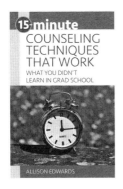

15-MINUTE COUNSELING TECHNIQUES THAT WORK
What You Didn't Learn in Grad School

Allison Edwards

ANGER, RAGE, AND AGGRESSION

Dr. Raychelle Cassada Lohmann

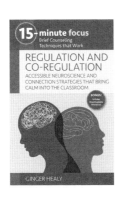

REGULATION AND CO-REGULATION
Accessible Neoroscience and Connection Strategies that Bring Calm Into the Classroom

Ginger Healy

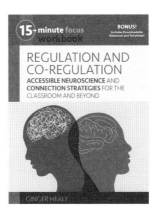

REGULATION AND CO-REGULATION WORKBOOK
Accessible Neoroscience and Connection Strategies for the Classroom and Beyond

Ginger Healy

15-MINUTE FOCUS
Anxiety Workbook: Tips and Strategies to Manage Anxiety, Build Resilience, and Foster Emotional Well-Being

213

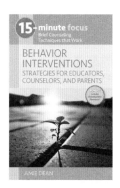

BEHAVIOR INTERVENTIONS
Strategies for Educators, Counselors, and Parents

Amie Dean

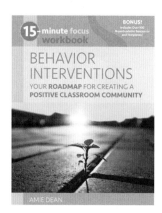

BEHAVIOR INTERVENTIONS WORKBOOK
Your Roadmap for Creating a Positive Classroom Community

Amie Dean

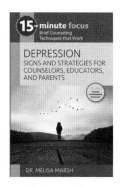

DEPRESSION
Signs and Strategies for Counselors, Educators, and Parents

Dr. Melisa Marsh

DIGITAL CITIZENSHIP
Supporting Youth Navigating Technology in a Rapidly Changing World

Dr. Raychelle Cassada Lohmann and Dr. Angie Smith

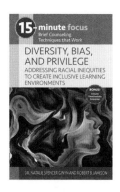

DIVERSITY, BIAS, AND PRIVILEGE
Addressing Racial Inequities to Create Inclusive Learning Environments

Dr. Natalie Spencer Gwyn and Robert B. Jamison

GRIEF
Processing and Recovery

David A. Opalewski, M.A.

214

15-MINUTE FOCUS
Anxiety Workbook: Tips and Strategies to Manage Anxiety, Build Resilience, and Foster Emotional Well-Being

GROWTH MINDSET, RESILIENCE, AND GRIT
Harnessing Internal Superpowers
for Student Success

Dr. Raychelle Cassada Lohmann

BEHAVIORAL THREAT ASSESSMENT
AND MANAGEMENT
for K-12 Schools

Dr. Melissa A. Louvar Reeves

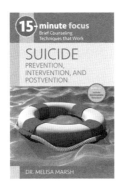

SUICIDE
Prevention, Intervention, and Postvention

Dr. Melisa Marsh

TRAUMA
and Adverse Childhood Experiences

Dr. Melissa A. Louvar Reeves

15-MINUTE FOCUS
Anxiety Workbook: Tips and Strategies to Manage Anxiety, Build Resilience, and Foster Emotional Well-Being

215

About NCYI

National Center for Youth Issues provides educational resources, training, and support programs to foster the healthy social, emotional, and physical development of children and youth. Since our founding in 1981, NCYI has established a reputation as one of the country's leading providers of teaching materials and training for counseling and student-support professionals. NCYI helps meet the immediate needs of students throughout the nation by ensuring those who mentor them are well prepared to respond across the developmental spectrum.

Connect With Us Online!

@nationalcenterforyouthissues

@ncyi

@nationalcenterforyouthissues

216

15-MINUTE FOCUS
Anxiety Workbook: Tips and Strategies to Manage Anxiety, Build Resilience, and Foster Emotional Well-Being